HUTS FULL OF CHARACTER

52 Charming Huts in the Alps

Like a bird's nest, the Rifugio Nuvolau crowns the summit and, with the rugged rocks, it is bathed in golden light by the sun.

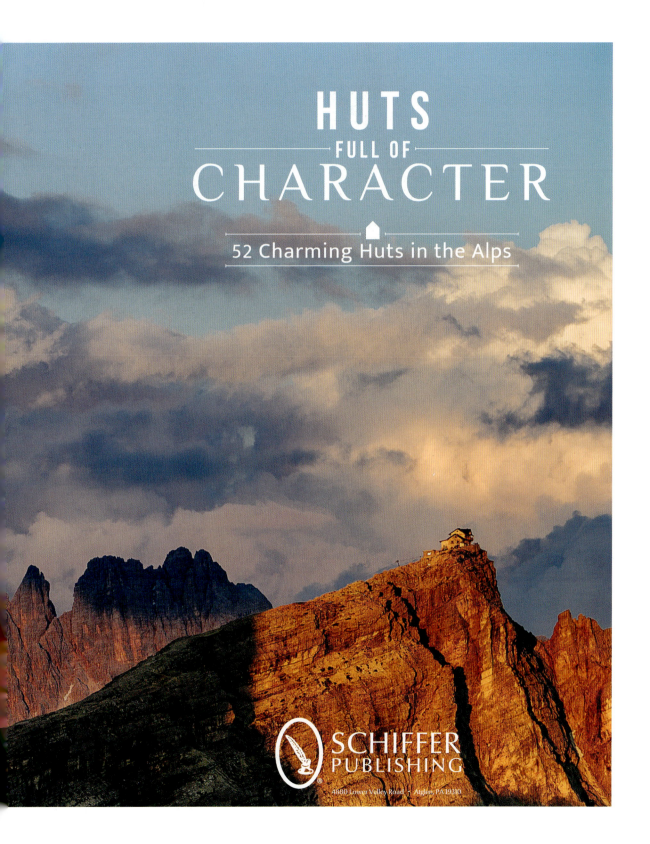

TABLE OF CONTENTS

TABLE OF CONTENTS

Overview map of the Alps		6
Preface		8
Hut rules		10

🇫🇷 FRANCE — 14
1	Refuge du Pelvoux	16
2	Auberge du Truc	22
3	Refuge de Tête Rousse	28
4	Refuge des Cosmiques	32
5	Refuge du Couvercle	36

🇨🇭 SWITZERLAND — 44
6	Doldenhornhütte	46
7	Fründenhütte	50
8	Blüemlisalphütte	56
9	Mischabelhütte	62
10	Gaulihütte	68
11	Capanna Corno Gries	74
12	Sewenhütte	80
13	Terrihütte	86
14	Berggasthaus Schäfler	92

🇱🇮 LIECHTENSTEIN — 98
| 15 | Pfälzerhütte | 100 |

🇩🇪 GERMANY — 104
16	Waltenbergerhaus	106
17	Reintalangerhütte	110
18	Weilheimer Hütte	116
19	Soiernhaus	122
20	Tegernseer Hütte	128
21	Reichenhaller Haus	134

🇦🇹 AUSTRIA — 140
22	Saarbrücker Hütte	142
23	Kaltenberghütte	148
24	Brandenburger Haus	154
25	Rüsselsheimer Hütte	160
26	Ramolhaus	166
27	Coburger Hütte	170
28	Winnebachseehütte	174
29	Siegerlandhütte	180
30	Franz-Senn-Hütte	184
31	Nürnberger Hütte	188
32	Falkenhütte	192
33	Gamshütte	198
34	Berliner Hütte	204
35	Greizer Hütte	208
36	Anton-Karg-Haus	214
37	Stüdlhütte	218
38	Salmhütte	224

🇮🇹 ITALY — 230
39	Rifugio Lobbia Alta	232
40	Düsseldorfer Hütte (Rifugio Serristori)	238
41	Zufallhütte (Rifugio Nino Corsi)	246
42	Müllerhütte (Rifugio Cima Libera)	252
43	Flaggerschartenhütte (Rifugio Forcella Vallaga)	258
44	Schlernhaus (Rifugio Bolzano)	266
45	Gartlhütte (Rifugio Re Alberto I)	272
46	Tierser Alpl Hütte (Rifugio Alpe di Tires)	278
47	Brixner Hütte (Rifugio Bressanone)	282
48	Pisciadù Hütte (Rifugio Franco Cavazza al Pisciadù)	288
49	Rifugio Nuvolau	296
50	Büllelejochhütte (Rifugio Pian di Cengia)	302

🇸🇮 SLOVENIA — 308
| 51 | Koča pri Triglavskih jezerih | 310 |
| 52 | Češka Koča | 316 |

Index	324
Picture credits	328
Imprint	328

There isn't much that compares to the feeling that overcomes you when you look down into the valley from the window of a hut after a successful climb.

ALPS | OVERVIEW MAP

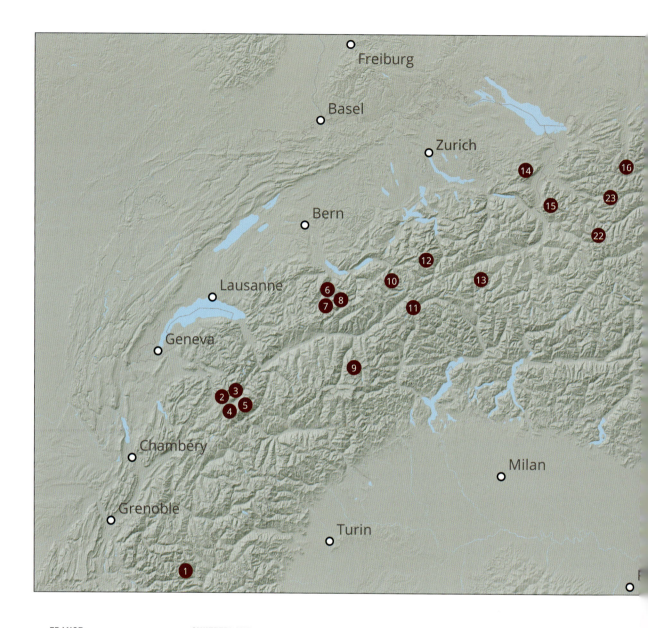

🇫🇷 FRANCE
1 Refuge du Pelvoux
2 Auberge du Truc
3 Refuge de Tête Rousse
4 Refuge des Cosmiques
5 Refuge du Couvercle

🇨🇭 SWITZERLAND
6 Doldenhornhütte
7 Fründenhütte
8 Blüemlisalphütte
9 Mischabelhütte
10 Gaulihütte
11 Capanna Corno Gries
12 Sewenhütte
13 Terrihütte

14 Berggasthaus Schäfler

🇱🇮 LIECHTENSTEIN
15 Pfälzerhütte

🇩🇪 GERMANY
16 Waltenbergerhaus
17 Reintalangerhütte
18 Weilheimer Hütte

19 Soiernhaus
20 Tegernseer Hütte
21 Reichenhaller Haus

🇦🇹 AUSTRIA
22 Saarbrücker Hütte
23 Kaltenberghütte
24 Brandenburger Haus
25 Rüsselsheimer Hütte

OVERVIEW MAP | ALPS

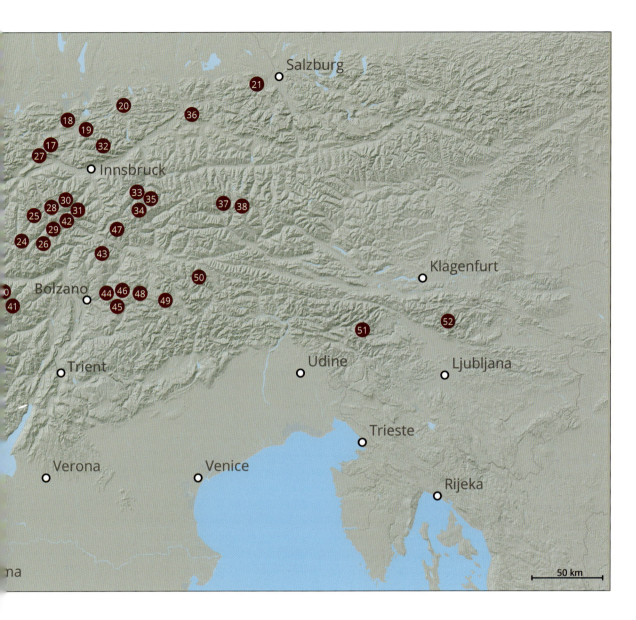

26 Ramolhaus	**35** Greizer Hütte	**42** Müllerhütte	**SLOVENIA**
27 Coburger Hütte	**36** Anton-Karg-Haus	**43** Flaggerschartenhütte	**51** Koca pri Triglavskih
28 Winnebachseehütte	**37** Stüdlhütte	**44** Schlernhaus	jezerih
29 Siegerlandhütte	**38** Salmhütte	**45** Gartlhütte	**52** Česka Koča
30 Franz-Senn-Hütte		**46** Tierser Alpl Hütte	
31 Nürnberger Hütte	**ITALY**	**47** Brixner Hütte	
32 Falkenhütte	**39** Rifugio Lobbia Alta	**48** Pisciaduhütte	
33 Gamshütte	**40** Düsseldorfer Hütte	**49** Rifugio Nuvolau	
34 Berliner Hütte	**41** Zufallhütte	**50** Büllelejochhütte	

PREFACE

Anything but ordinary

If you've seen one, have you seen them all? Absolutely not if you're talking about Alpine huts! From small to spacious, old-fashioned to avant-garde, from easy-to-reach to reserved for ambitious athletes.

There are many reasons why none of the more than 60 hosted huts in the Alps from France to Slovenia is like any other. Their locations alone make each hut unique: One is visible from afar on an exposed rocky outcrop, while others are hidden in peaceful pine forests. What's inside them lends each Alpine hut its own special character. Whether it's a particularly cozy lounge, the host team's warm hospitality, or the local culinary delights: when the chemistry is right, they take guests' hearts by storm.

However, the conditions must be right for this. That's why the icons in this book tell you more about each hut: whether it is child-friendly, for example, or whether it pays attention to sustainability.

A few crucial facts and figures about the huts are presented in the "In Brief" boxes. Markus and Janina Meier give potential hikers the real scoop with anecdotes from their hiking diary. Readers who are considering hiking in the Alps can find inspiration in the suggested hiking routes. The starting point is usually at or near the hut; altitude information applies only for the ascent.

Are you ready for adventure?
Then head for the mountains! ❄

You've packed your backpack, laced up your hiking boots, and selected a hut as your destination. What else do you need? Right: a good friend who will come along and share the adventure.

THE RIGHT ONE FOR YOU

- **Hut with a view** Just take a deep breath and be amazed.
- **Adventure included** In most cases, the ascent is already challenging.
- **Gourmet hut** Culinary enjoyment to the max.
- **Suitable for children** No one will be bored here.
- **Sustainable** Especially sparing use of natural resources.

PREFACE

HUT RULES

HUT RULES

Shoes can start to stink after a strenuous climb. So it's good that you don't have to take them where you'll be sleeping; you can store them in the shoe rooms.

Better together

When you head for the mountains, it's pure pleasure! With good preparation and a little forethought, every hut holiday becomes a relaxing all-round experience.

1. RESERVE & CANCEL

When it comes to an overnight stay in a hut, you can check off the first to-do item on your list from the valley: Reserve a bed. Especially in the high season, many huts are crowded and often booked out several days in advance. If you have a specific date in mind, it's a good idea to register early. In most cases, a call or an e-mail will do the trick. In the meantime, some DAV (Deutscher Alpenverein—German Alpine Club) huts offer online reservations with a traffic light system that indicates whether or not there is availability during a selected period. Very important: If something comes up and you won't need the bed, be sure to cancel your reservation. Tired hiking enthusiasts will be grateful.

2. PAY CASH & BE GENEROUS

Cash is king, and in the mountains this is still true today. Online payment systems require stable reception, and that's not always a given in remote and high places. If you bring enough cash with you, you'll save yourself and the host a lot of trouble. And there's another consideration as well: Hikers who can afford to be generous can express their appreciation of the hosting team. After all, they put a lot of energy and effort into their daily work on the mountain. And a tip is not only measured by what it can buy.

11

HUT RULES

3. LEAVE YOUR MARK
No, this does not mean carving your initials into the wood. Instead, leave an entry in the hut's guestbook. What many see as a nice gesture can actually save lives. In addition to a friendly message, you should indicate which route you planned to take and when you left. If there's an emergency and you need help, you'll make the work of the emergency services personnel much easier with this information.

4. ENJOY YOUR MEAL
… because what's put on the table is almost always fresh, regional, and delicious. As a guest at the hut, it's important to keep in mind that managing a hut is a feat of strength. Everything that is used here must be carefully selected, ordered in advance, and painstakingly transported. Please don't make any special requests for food that are not medically necessary. By the way, most huts have fixed meal times that you should be aware of and adhere to. Who wants to go to bed hungry and miss the fun of eating together?

5. ARE YOU WILLING TO HELP? THAT'S A PLUS
Especially in small huts, the atmosphere is very homey: You get to know each other, you talk, you eat together. Why not clean up together after dinner? Assisting the host team with small everyday tasks doesn't take a lot of effort, and it's nice recognition. If you help, then at the end of the day there may be more time to enjoy the friendly atmosphere.

6. A PLACE IN THE SUN
A towel as a placeholder on a lounge chair or a backpack to reserve the largest table? Please don't do this! If you ask kindly, everyone will cuddle up a bit. That way, there's space for everyone in even the smallest hut.

7. SHHHH!
One of the main reasons for a trip to the mountains: The heavenly peace! Together, we can preserve the peace and fight the noise. With a bit of empathetic consideration, this isn't that difficult. Many mountaineers leave in the middle of the night, so they go to bed early. Those who want to stay up longer should talk quietly, not play any loud music, and creep into their beds, if possible without disturbing anyone (see point 8). Please remember: Wooden huts are not usually soundproofed. Earplugs are recommended, especially for those who sleep in shared rooms or dormitories, for there's nothing else to do about those who snore.

8. FLASHLIGHT VS. STUMBLING IN THE DARK
A headlamp or small flashlight is an absolute must for every overnight stay in a hut! It's not just for your personal well-being if you can provide your own lighting for the washbasin. And your roommates in the dormitory will appreciate it if you creep into your sleeping bag instead of rattling and stumbling to your bed.

9. NO STINKY BOOTS WHERE YOU SLEEP
Anyone who has worn their hiking boots all day knows what to expect when taking them off: They don't exactly smell like roses. In each hut there is special place for airing out hiking and ski boots—and of course it's not where you'll be sleeping. Leave your stinky shoes outside the door, and thank goodness, everyone will do the same.

10. WI-FI? GO OFFLINE FOR A CHANGE
The nature, quiet, and fresh air are all so beautiful —but why isn't there any Internet here?! Just relax and use your trip to the mountains as a "digital detox" period. Even though some mountain huts now have WiFi reception, it's not a matter of course, and sometimes it doesn't suit the hut hosts' philosophy. So a little time offline is consciously part of enjoying the mountains and all your senses have time to enjoy the gift of the mountains.

You don't have to be "on" all the time and everywhere—especially not when the landscape invites you to take a breath and switch off for a change.
"Please switch off your mobile phone here."

Warm blankets and pillows are usually available for guests, as here in the Forno Hütte. You must bring a hut sleeping bag along.

HUT RULES

PACKING LIST
Recommended by the German Alpine Association

- Sleeping bag or hut sleeping bag, sheets, pillowcase (as of June 2020, please inquire at the hut)
- Headlamp or small flashlight (if you have to get up at night)
- Earplugs for a quiet night
- DAV membership card
- Hut and/or house slippers
- Small towel (ideally a microfiber towel: Small, lightweight, and quick-drying)
- Wash bag with toothbrush, toothpaste, small soap/shower gel, deodorant

 FRANCE

Europe's highest peak is in France, so it should come as no surprise that the country, and especially the Mont Blanc massif, is on many mountaineers' to-do lists. That's why this region has many huts and trails, so that if you are fit enough and have plenty of experience and strength, you can tackle the ascent of the "highest one." For those adventurers for whom even a simple mountain hut provides too much comfort, some huts will also allow you to pitch a tent on their premises. If you don't want to go too high or you're curious about what else the French part of the Alps has to offer, you can visit the Refuge du Pelvoux, for example. It is located in the fascinating landscape of the Dauphiné Alps.

When the peaks of the Mont Blanc massif protrude even higher than the clouds, the sun makes its snow and ice caps sparkle.

FRANCE | PROVENCE-ALPS-CÔTE D'AZURE

1

The Distant One

REFUGE DU PELVOUX The Refuge du Pelvoux is in the wild Dauphiné Alps. It's a long way from Ailefroide to the hut. But the journey is worthwhile, the landscape is magnificent, and towering above the hut is the eponymous Mont Pelvoux, which offers a fabulous crossing in this southwest part of the Alps.

It's a beautiful morning on a bright summer day. We are sitting comfortably at the campsite in Ailefroide and waiting for our mountain guide. We are in the Dauphiné Alps, a wild mountain range in the southwest Alps. It has long been our dream to visit this region.

It's a long way from lovely Ailefroide to the Refuge du Pelvoux. After passing through a beautiful larch forest, we hike across open terrain. The midday sun shines down on us relentlessly. We leave ourselves plenty of time and enjoy the magnificent scenery. When we arrive at the hut, we are happy that our mountain guide speaks good French and for the water that is sold up here.

This simple stone structure was built below the summit cliffs of Mont Pelvoux in 1962. But with the Refuge du Provence (built in 1877) and its new building, the Refuge Lemercier, which was built in 1892, the area had several mountain huts even before the Refuge du Pelvoux was built. The Refuge serves as the base camp for Mont Pelvoux. This massif is unfamiliar to many people. Most hikers travel here to scale the only 13,000-foot peak in the Dauphiné, the Barre des

←

The Refuge du Pelvoux blends perfectly into its surroundings in terms of more than just colour. Despite its practical nature, the hut looks very inviting, especially after the ascent.

17

FRANCE | PROVENCE-ALPS-CÔTE D'AZUR | REFUGE DU PELVOUX

Écrins. But crossing its southeastern neighbor is also a special experience, one worth having at least once.

Anyone traveling here will be happy about even the simplest hut. Just a cursory glance at the Refuge indicates that you would be looking in vain for luxury here. The sturdy building seems to be trying to keep pace with the rough peaks surrounding it, and the hut looks like the proverbial rock in the surf—only the sea is missing. Just so you know, the building material was transported to this remote location by helicopter. The hut's interior is furnished in a practical style, and it offers only the essential comforts.

However, the reception is warm, and there is hearty food prepared by Mat and his kitchen team, which provides necessary refreshment after the strenuous hike. Omelets, pasta, and soup—the ingredients vary from day to day. And naturally there is French wine.

IN BRIEF

VALLEY TOWN Ailefroide

ALTITUDE 8,871 ft/2,704 m above sea level

OPEN beginning of May to mid-September

ACCOMMODATIONS 54 beds in shared rooms, winter camp with facilities for 10 people

FOOD Simple French cuisine

GOOD TO KNOW The long climb makes you thirsty, so you should be sure to take enough water along.

18

REFUGE DU PELVOUX | PROVENCE-ALPS-CÔTE D'AZURE | FRANCE

The reflection in a clear mountain lake doubles the alpine glow of Mont Pelvoux.

Anyone who takes on the peaks of the massif deserves a moment of jubilation.

After a night that seems much too short, we make our way to the summit of Mont Pelvoux. As soon as we leave the hut, it's time to get down to business. We scale the first crest by the light of our headlamps. A short while later, we will head to the famous Coolidge Couloir, which is an ice chute that requires confident crampon hiking. These days, this climb is only possible in early summer. The Couloir is named for the British climber who was the first person to scale the Jungfrau in the Bernese Oberland. At the top of Mont Pelvoux, the view is fantastic; it reminds us that even mountains below the magical four-thousand-foot mark are worthwhile destinations.

The hut's special location involves some difficulties. The water supply is adjusted annually to suit current conditions. That's why the pipeline must be reinstalled each year. Access for workers is only possible via a fixed-rope route, which is why it's important to conserve water in the hut. Mountaineers are also asked to take some trash down with them into the valley for disposal.

TOURS

TOUR 1 CLIMBING ROUTE
Spectacular views: Ailefroide → Travers du Pelvoux and the Super Oin-Oin.
» 1,640 ft/500 m EG » 2.11 mi/3.4 km
» 7.5 hrs. » difficult

TOUR 2 MONT PELVOUX
Scale both peaks of Mont Pelvoux. Climbing required, and a difficult trail due to the scree.
» 4,229 ft/1,289 m EG » 4.85 mi/7.8 km
» 3.5 hrs. » difficult

TOUR 3 CROSSING M. PELVOUX
From the Refuge across the Clot de l'Homme, Sialouze, and Pelvoux glaciers, then from Névé Pélissier to Ailefroide.
» 4,196 ft/1,279 m EG
» 6.34 mi/10.2km » 9.5 hrs. » difficult

FRANCE | PROVENCE-ALPS-CÔTE D'AZURE | REFUGE DU PELVOUX

Climbing in Ailefroid

Ailefroide not only has a nice campsite, it also offers several beautiful climbing routes near the valley. The access routes are really short, but the climbing routes can be as long as 15 pitches and cross the best granite. There is probably no other place in the Alps with so many great climbing routes so close by. Here it is worth not only planning a high-altitude tour, but also taking a climbing holiday.

→

Both muscle strength and the greatest concentration are required when climbing. It's precisely this mixture that makes climbing an intense experience.

REFUGE DU PELVOUX | PROVENCE-ALPS-CÔTE D'AZURE | FRANCE

FRANCE | AUVERGNE-RHÔNE-ALPES

On the Monarch

AUBERGE DU TRUC When Bernadette saw the faces of her awed guests, she just smiled and often asked mischievously: "It's quite a nice backdrop we have, isn't it?" Because the panorama from the Auberge du Truc is almost too glorious to be true. Today, her two children operate the hut—but the magnificent view is still the same, of course. And hikers also appreciate the hut's purist flair.

Of course, it's not a backdrop that surrounds the hut, but the 360° view is quite picturesque. It extends from the glacial Dômes de Miage to the Chaîne des Aravis. Although the hut can be reached easily from the valley, most guests probably take a different route to get there, for the famous Tour du Mont-Blanc runs right past the Auberge du Truc. And anyone who is on the way to this monarch of the Alps also appreciates simple things: An authentic feeling in the hut, the community in the bunk rooms, the refreshing water directly from the mountain, and an invigorating meal such as a hearty omelet with sausage and cheese. And by the way, the cheese is actually from here, as is the milk for the cheese. The family that operates the Auberge du Truc has also owned an alpine pasture for over 70 years. The animals graze right next to the hut, so you can learn a lot about how to manage a high-altitude pasture and sometimes even lend a hand while you're staying there. And if you drink a glass of fresh milk or try a curd dish, you will taste the difference—these products are

It's not just the colorful flower pots that make the Auberge du Truc seem inviting, but also its gentle contrast to the imposing but rugged peaks around it.

🇫🇷 FRANCE | AUVERGNE-RHÔNE-ALPES | AUBERGE DU TRUC

IN BRIEF

VALLEY TOWN Saint-Gervais-les-Bains

ALTITUDE 5,741 ft/1,750 m above sea level

OPEN mid-June to mid-September

ACCOMMODATIONS 28 beds

FOOD Breakfast, lunch, and dinner are simple and good; homemade berry tarts; dairy products made in-house; box lunches on request

GOOD TO KNOW There is cold running water, but there are no showers - so be sure to bring a washcloth.

straight from the meadow next door. Breakfast at the Auberge du Truc is simple and consists of bread, butter, and jam. However, you will have plenty of strength to start the day. If you want to, you can order a box lunch, so that you won't run out of energy when you're on your way to the monarch or back to the valley.

And speaking of energy: Some people may wonder how, in this beautiful mountain landscape, it's possible to supply electricity and water to a hut. The Auberge du Truc has chosen a sustainable solution. The hut uses rainwater and has a solar system to generate electricity. On the subject of water, it's worth mentioning that the spring that the hut once used was drying out, so people decided not to take showers. There is cold running water and there are sinks, so a sponge bath will have to do. Overnight guests should bring a hut sleeping bag—but if you forget, sleeping bags are for sale in the Auberge.

Hosts Martine and Jean-Philippe are great assets of the Auberge du Truc. Both of them grew up in the hut and they know the area, the

AUBERGE DU TRUC | AUVERGNE-RHÔNE-ALPES | FRANCE

animals, and life in the mountain pasture intimately. Their welcome is warm and it echoes the hut's free mountain spirit.

When the sun is shining here, there's no better place to be than just sitting in the meadow near the hut and relaxing. All the stresses of hiking and everyday life blow away in the wind, which gently stirs the blades of grass and flowers. And if the weather is rough, the toasty stove bench inside the hut is a favorite spot for hikers. Nowhere in the Auberge du Truc is it as cozy as it is here!

TOURS

TOUR 1 REFUGE DE LA BALME
Hiking from hut to hut is more fun than going back the way you came. This is a scenic hike: Auberge du Truc → Refuge de la Balme, through the Contamines-Montjoie Nature Reserve and across the Tête Noire.
» 2,329 ft/710 m EG » 8.76 mi/14.1 km
» 6 h » medium

TOUR 2 TOUR DU MONT BLANC
This is the most famous tour, and it is well-marked; the Auberge du Truc is a good place to stop. The next day, you will hike through coniferous forests to Les Contamines and through the Bonnant valley toward Refuge de la Balme before climbing the Col de la Croix Bonhomme to the Refuge de la Croix Bonhomme.
» 4,429 ft/1,350 m EG » 11.43 mi/18.4 km
» 7 h » difficult

↓

As if the chain of snow-capped peaks were not enough on its own, the scenery is also reflected in the water of the Lacs des Chéserys, as is the radiant blue sky.

25

FRANCE | AUVERGNE-RHÔNE-ALPES | AUBERGE DU TRUC

Night-time wonder

Who hasn't experienced this: You wake up in the middle of the night and have to use the toilet. First you try to fall asleep again, then you decide to get out of your warm bed. Carefully, you make your way to the door. Then you step outside. Wow, it's nippy up here! And the outdoor toilet is about 330 feet away. But going back to bed? Not an option. So you scurry out and hurry toward the toilet. Only on the way back, when your thoughts aren't focused on your bladder but rather on this quiet place, do you look up as if by chance. And you stop in your tracks. You've forgotten the cold, your warm bed can wait. Thousands of stars twinkle in the sky. Sometimes it's actually worth leaving your warm sleeping bag at night.

→ Often, the cities around us are far too bright to see a really great starry sky. However, things are completely different in the mountains!

AUBERGE DU TRUC | AUVERGNE-RHÔNE-ALPES | FRANCE 🇫🇷

FRANCE | AUVERGNE-RHÔNE-ALPES

The Panoramic Window

← Yes, mountain huts can also be quite modern. A good example is the Refuge de Tête Rousse, which is surrounded by cliffs and scree.

REFUGE DE TÊTE ROUSSE The normal route to Mont Blanc, a mountain peak in the Alps that is almost mythical for mountaineers, follows the Goûter Route. Anyone who sets out to conquer the "roof of Europe" must be prepared for the elevation gain. A stop at the Refuge, which is at 10,390 ft/3,167 m, makes it easier to acclimatize in the unusually thin air. Time positively flies by when you look out the hut's big windows at the breathtaking mountain scenery all around you.

The Refuge de la Tête Rousse has very large windows. Since the beginning of the 2000s, this modern hut has stood below the north face of the Aiguille de Bionnassay in the French Mont Blanc massif. The new building solved an old, familiar problem on heavily frequented alpine routes: The old building could no longer accommodate the influx of visitors; it was bursting at the seams. During the season, numerous alpinists are drawn to this heavily touristed region, where the "Tramway de Mont Blanc" cogwheel railway has been making the trip up the mountain child's play for over 100 years. Sitting comfortably and with a lot of nostalgic flair, it climbs up to a height of 7,545 feet at the Nid d'Aigle terminal station on the Glacier de Bionnassay. However, the approximately two-hour-long march from there to the hut is reserved for sports enthusiasts because you are in a high alpine environment—including all the challenges

FRANCE | AUVERGNE-RHÔNE-ALPES | REFUGE DE TÊTE ROUSSE

associated with this. And dangers. The 1892 accident on the Tête Rousse Glacier demonstrates how powerful and unavoidable catastrophes can be. Hidden under a thick layer of ice, melt water had pooled unnoticed over time, forming a huge glacial lake. On the night of July 12, the ice broke under enormous pressure, a huge tidal wave rushed into the valley and surprised the sleeping inhabitants of Saint Gervais. Many had no chance to escape. Admittedly, this was a once-in-a-century event. Warnings about dangerous falling rock on the normal route, however, cannot be repeated often enough - even today.

At the hut's campsite, it even feels a bit like you're in the Himalayas. Hard-bitten people who have trained for high altitude can set up their night camp on the wooden terraces around the hut. If you prefer sleeping someplace warmer than in the high alpine cold, you can reserve a bed inside the hut.

IN BRIEF

VALLEY TOWN Saint-Gervais-les-Bains

ALTITUDE 10,390 ft/3,167 m above sea level

OPEN June to September

ACCOMMODATIONS 72 beds

FOOD simple but high-quality food; snack bar from 9 AM to 4 PM; dinner for everyone at 6:30 PM; there are two times for breakfast (4 AM and 7 AM)

GOOD TO KNOW Your own bed sheet or hut sleeping bag is required. There is no running water in the hut.

REFUGE DE ROUSSE | AUVERGNE-RHÔNE-ALPES | FRANCE

Surefootedness is also required when hiking in the Mont Blanc massif if the ground is stony.

From the Aiguille du Midi, there is an impressive full view of the Mont Blanc massif.

The hut team managed by Léo Bocher and Antoine Rattin will always keep your feet warm; they provide each guest with slippers. They are not only responsible for making sure things run smoothly here, they also manage the Nid d'Aigle and Goûter huts. Those who make their way from the Refuge to the latter sometimes have a dangerous passage along the Aiguille du Goûter Couloir—keyword, falling rock. A conversation with the hut hosts and mountain guides before you set out will help you correctly assess the current situation and wait for suitable conditions. And it's no problem if they keep you waiting: A cup of cappuccino and a giant chocolate cookie on the sun terrace can make up for many delays. In general: Don't the clocks up here tick quite differently anyway?

TOURS

TOUR 1 AIGUILLE DE BIONNASSAY
The Bionnassay glacier is very close to the hut. Cross it, and you will be climbing the NW flank of the Aiguille de Bionnassay.
» 2,903 ft/885 m EG   » 1.86 mi/3 km
» 5,5 h   » difficult

TOUR 2 MONT BLANC
Stop at the the Refuges Goûter and Vallot on the way to Mont Blanc.
» 7,867 ft/2,398 m EG   » 7.95mi/12.8 km
» 8 h   » difficult

TOUR 3 AIGUILLE DU GOÛTER
If Mont Blanc isn't for you, try the Aiguille de Goûter via the Grand Couloir to the eponymous Refuge.
» 4,790 ft/1,460 m EG   » 1.11mi/1.8 km
» 3 h   » difficult

FRANCE | AUVERGNE-RHÔNE-ALPES

4

The Researcher

One can only marvel at the idiosyncratic architecture of the Refuge des Cosmiques, which looks a bit like the nests that coastal birds build on steep cliffs.

REFUGE DES COSMIQUES There is a direct connection between space and France's second highest hut, and not only because a French astrophysicist built it in the 1930s to study cosmic radiation. When the cloud cover spreads over the rest of the world below the hut as it does some days, you feel far, far away from anything earthly.

However, the original hut, from which research was done up to the 1990s into the subject of air pollution and other topics, is gone. It burned down a few years ago. The new, modern structure of glass and dark wood blends so seamlessly into the rugged cliffs of the Mont Blanc massif that you might even mistake it for a rock. The hut is surrounded by a magical world of snow and ice in the summer and winter. To the west is the Glacier des Bossons, to the east the Vallée Blanche, the "white valley," a popular destination for ambitious skiers. Mountaineers like to use the Refuge as a base on their route to Mont Blanc (15,780 feet), the legendary "roof of Europe." The so-called Cosmique route, off the beaten track, leads across the Col du Midi, the northern flank of Mont Blanc du Tacul, and the Col du Mont Maudit to the highest mountain in the Alps. At the latest, when its name is spoken, it's clear: This region is an alpine high mountain range. Without technical skills and good conditioning, life quickly becomes dangerous up here. Alpine experience is also required for the relatively easy access to the hut via the Aiguille du Midi. From Chamonix, you can re-

33

FRANCE | AUVERGNE-RHÔNE-ALPES | REFUGE DES COSMIQUES

ach the top of this rocky peak by cable car in 20 minutes. From there, the path involves an elevation gain of about 650 feet over the ridge down to the Refuge.

If you are not used to the thin air at high altitude, acclimatize yourself there first. The gigantic view of the grandiose mountain world will keep you occupied. A place in front of the wide windows in the common room is ideal when wind and weather roar outside. If the weather is clear, the expansive terraces will lure you outdoors.

Essential supplies are delivered by helicopter at regular intervals: But because landing here is impossible, the host team takes their deliveries dangling on long ropes. Those who are lucky enough to be staying at the hut on a delivery day will be impressed by the pilots' skills and will probably appreciate the good food afterwards all the more.

The hut is operated by the Chamonix Mountain Guide Association, but Mélanie and Noé

IN BRIEF

VALLEY TOWN Chamonix

ALTITUDE 11,854 ft/3,613 m above sea level

OPEN February to September

ACCOMMODATIONS 130-bed dormitory; winter room with 10 beds

FOOD half-board with dinner and breakfast or dishes à la carte

GOOD TO KNOW water is scarce here, so there are no showers, but there is cellular service. Pay in cash or by card.

34

REFUGE DES COSMIQUES | AUVERGNE-RHÔNE-ALPES | FRANCE

As the crow flies, Mont Blanc du Tacul awaits daring and experienced climbers about 1.3 km from the hut.

take care of management on site. They spend most of the year here, conjuring up warm and tasty food from simple ingredients, filling hungry mountaineers' stomachs, and they are always available for questions about mountains and sport. For they would not live the life of privation in this unique world if they were not truly passionate about the high mountains. They get to experience the magic of a world that doesn't exist anywhere else, one that they enjoy sharing with guests at the Refuge. And thus, we have returned to the cosmos that gives the Refuge its name. Its greetings reach the earth first of all here, it seems.

TOURS

TOUR 1 MONT BLANC
Climb Mont Blanc via the Cosmiques route. This tour is demanding and requires a lot of high-mountain experience. The signs are good, the most difficult part is the firn and ice flank below Mont Maudit to the shoulder. As you will climb the NW flank of Mont Blanc du Tacul in the dark, you should test this route beforehand.
» 5,338 ft/1,627 m EG   » 8.7 mi/14 km
» 13 h   » difficult

TOUR 2 AIGUILLE DU PLAN
From the hut: Col du Midi → Col du Plan. After a demanding rappelling stretch, continue to the Rognon du Plan and to the peak.
» 2,953 ft/900 m EG   » 3.85 mi/6.2 km
» 10 h   » difficult

Sunsets are always magical in the mountains, like here from Mont Blanc du Tacul.

35

FRANCE | AUVERGNE-RHÔNE-ALPES

5

The Demanding One

The Refuge du Couvercle looks just as massive as the rugged cliffs around it. On fine days it is busy, and everyone enjoys the view from the terrace.

REFUGE DU COUVERCLE The hike to Refuge du Couvercle is certainly not a leisurely walk up the mountain! After all, it lies directly on the Mont Blanc massif, below the peaks of the 13,123-foot Grandes Jorasses. So the tour leading to the hut is a challenge. Similarly, a stay at the Refuge du Couvercle is no picnic, but chances are that no brave climber in this region expects that.

After overcoming glaciers, elevation gains, and that voice inside your head (the one that sometimes tells you to turn around), you finally reach this hut at an altitude of 8,802 feet. It hardly stands out from its surroundings because it is built from the same gray stone. And it's not just its color that matches the landscape. It looks just as robust as the big boulders around it. However, the light blue shutters beckon invitingly, and so you will surely be tempted to bound up the last steps to the entrance.

And then? First of all, take off your sturdy shoes—it's a treat for your toes to move freely in the air again!—and exchange them for colorful clogs. They are mandatory inside the hut, and many pairs are available in various sizes right in the entrance hall. In the next room, you can finally shed more ballast, which was necessary on the hike, but will only be in your way in the hut because there are large boxes here where you can put your ice axes, crampons, etc. Now just register, and voilà, you're a guest at the Refuge du Couvercle. Keep in mind that things are not always easy in this exposed

FRANCE | AUVERGNE-RHÔNE-ALPES | REFUGE DU COUVERCLE

IN BRIEF

VALLEY TOWN Chamonix-Mont-Blanc

ALTITUDE 8,802 ft/2,683 m above sea level

OPEN from the beginning of April to the end of September

ACCOMMODATIONS 64 beds; when the hut isn't operating: 20 beds

FOOD Breakfast and dinner by request, drinks & small snacks during the day

GOOD TO KNOW Specify dietary requirements when booking

Especially when the sky is a friendly blue, the Aiguille du Moine is a destination worth recommending.

situation. For example, charging mobile phones. The hut's electricity is supplied by solar cells—at night and when the hut is full, you will not be able to recharge your mobile phone. There is no WiFi, so you can concentrate entirely on the here and now and talk to other hikers, and games and books are also available.

You will sleep in dormitories with between 16 and 25 beds; guests are housed according to when they plan to get up. It's also not easy to supply the hut with water. The water comes directly from the spring, but it's often hidden under snow and ice until well into spring, and even in summer, the collection containers that make water use possible frequently have to be repositioned. So life at the Refuge du Couvercle couldn't be much more authentic. The purist furnishings and the interior made mainly of wood also give this impression. Nothing else would suit the landscape surrounding The Demanding One. Rugged peaks, snow everywhere, colorful chains of flags fluttering in the harsh wind. You feel sublime and tiny when you're sitting with others in front of the hut in the eve-

REFUGE DU COUVERCLE | AUVERGNE-RHÔNE-ALPES | FRANCE

ning, watching the sun set slowly behind the jagged mountain ridges. Such a moment has a special magic. That's something of which the hosts of the Refuge, who like to quote the famous French climber Gaston Rébuffat, are also aware. Due to their absolute wildness and extreme lack of vegetation, he once described the mountains as a kingdom that is nevertheless priceless since money can't buy happiness.

TOURS

TOUR 1 AIGUILLE DU MOINE
The challenging Arête Sud Intégrale is a path that runs along the ridge.
» 2,378 ft/725 m EG   » 1.05 mi/1.7 km
» 6 h   » difficult

TOUR 2 MER DE GLACE
Chamonix → Montenvers → Mer de Glace. Be especially careful when descending from Montenvers to Mer de Glace via ladders.
» 6,158 ft/1,877 m EG   » 6.83 mi/11 km
» 7 h   » difficult

TOUR 3 LA NONNE
The S-N crossing features panoramic views and varied climbing
» 2,142 ft/653 m EG   » 6.52 mi/10.5 km
» 8 h   » medium

After a wintry shower, the "green needle," the Aiguille Verte, is suddenly no longer green, but powder-white.

🇫🇷 FRANCE | AUVERGNE-RHÔNE-ALPES | REFUGE DU COUVERCLE

Well-capped

Anyone regarding the Refuge du Couvercle for the first time should not be frightened. Because this older hut, which is now used only as winter accommodation, is directly beneath an enormous boulder. At first glance, you almost think it's falling directly onto the wooden hut clad in aluminum. But there's no reason to panic! The boulder is not moving and there is no danger to the hut, which was built in 1904. The granite block fell from the nearby Aiguille du Moine and came to rest in its protruding position—it lies over the hut like a lid. And that's what gave the Refuge du Couvercle its name, because the French word "couvercle" simply means "lid."

→ You might also think of the bizarre ensemble of hut and "rock lid" as if the hut were hiding under a large leaf like a beetle, seeking protection.

REFUGE DU COUVERCLE | AUVERGNE-RHÔNE-ALPES | FRANCE 🇫🇷

HUT BOOK

HUT BOOK

Architecture on the mountain

Shelters reconceived: Spectacular and controversial

Many Alpine huts were built over 100 years ago and the structures are now often dilapidated, so that renovation is no longer worthwhile. Then the only option is to tear down the old hut and build a new one. Today's requirements for a shelter differ significantly from those of the past, which is why some huts that were not to everyone's taste have been built in recent years. They bridge the gap between environmental sustainability, energy efficiency, and modern architecture. The Olpererhütte was one of the first huts to focus on climate-relevant construction, in 2006. A glass cube was added during atop the Capanna Corno Gries during atop its renovation. Other interesting new construction projects include the Monte Rosa Hut, the Schwarzensteinhütte, the Waltenberger Haus, and the Höllentalangerhütte.

Especially in the evening, when everything shimmers blue, the Monte Rosa hut shines, due not only to the splendor of its windows, but also its futuristic aura.

43

🇨🇭 SWITZERLAND

No other European country is as closely associated with mountains as Switzerland. And so it's no wonder that there are magnificent tours all over Switzerland; some easy, some exhausting, but always worthwhile. When they reach their destination, hikers can enjoy panoramic views that make them forget all their troubles.

And if the long views are not enough to recharge hikers' batteries, the best hospitality is available in the various huts. Cheese is the star here, but many other dishes are homemade with a sense of tradition.

Many huts also welcome young mountain climbers, which is why a hiking tour with the whole family is an option.
Reaching other huts requires excellent physical fitness.

The reflection of the Matterhorn in Lake Riffel is an impressive natural spectacle.

SWITZERLAND | BERN

The Flying Hut

DOLDENHORNHÜTTE The small, family-friendly Doldenhornhütte is located on a rocky outcrop high above Lake Oeschinen near Kandersteg, and it looks up at the mighty, 11,935-foot-high Doldenhorn that gives it its name. The hut is ideal for a flight with a paraglider due to its exposed location, and to encourage this, the hut owners have hung a windsock in the launch area.

It's still early in the morning, and we are just starting our descent from the imposing Doldenhorn. Our crampons grip well in hard snow, but hiking here requires caution. We look into the valley and the view feels almost vertical. The terrain is very steep. Far below the glacier, we look directly at the beautifully situated Lake Oeschinen.

The day before we climbed up to the Doldenhornhütte. In contrast to the trail to the summit, the hut trail is relaxed and varied. First there's the gravel road from Kandersteg toward Lake Oeschinen, then to the Bärentritt, where we hike holding onto a wire rope for a short distance. Then comes the magical path through larch and pine forests up to the little Doldenhornhütte, which is located on a beautiful meadow slope high above Lake Oeschinen.

We enjoy the afternoon on the sunny hut terrace and treat ourselves to a piece of Alpine cheese and a cold beer. There isn't much space here, but the hut is very cozy and you'll soon find yourself talking to the people sharing your table. We visit the paraglider launch site and

← It's not just the surroundings, which are not as gray and barren as many at high altitudes, that give the Doldenhornhütte an inviting flair.

SWITZERLAND | BERN | DOLDENHORNHÜTTE

are impressed by the pilots' daring. The hut is well worth a day trip due to its location, excellent hospitality, and the relatively short climb. If you want to travel really light, you can even have your backpack transported to the hut in the material cableway. It's also possible to make a nice round trip out of the hut hike. To do this, take the gravel road for the ascent from Kandersteg, then return to the Doldenhornhütte and descend back into the valley on the normal hut trail. However, this trail is quite exposed at one point and requires caution.

Anyone who plans to take on the Doldenhorn the next day must go to bed early. Your alarm clock will ring early, and it's almost a shame not to have more time to enjoy the delicious breakfast, but the mountain is calling. At 11,935 feet, it's a proper peak in the Bernese Alps, especially since the Doldenhornhütte is not even at 6,561 feet.

IN BRIEF

VALLEY TOWN Kandersteg

ALTITUDE 6,282 ft/1,915 m above sea level

OPEN June to September

ACCOMMODATIONS 38 beds in dormitories, winter room with 10 beds, all beds have duvets and pillows

FOOD simple Swiss cuisine, half board

GOOD TO KNOW For a hut hike, be sure to take the round-trip route. Toilet is located outside the hut

DOLDENHORNHÜTTE | BERN | SWITZERLAND

Look for the bright yellow bear's ear along the trail. (top)

The water rushes down the steep rock face near Kandersteg. (below)

That leaves over 5,577 feet to the summit. Nevertheless, the ascent across a steep glacier is a real pleasure, not least because of the spectacular panoramic view of the other famous mountains in the Bernese Alps. The neighboring peaks are particularly impressive: The enchanted Blüemlisalphorn and the Balmhorn with the Altels. Back at the hut, you can raise a glass to your journey to the summit and enjoy a mountaineer burger or Heidi's spätzli.

Unfortunately, we are not paragliders. Therefore, after another night, we can't take the direct shortcut to the valley, so we'll have to hike the footpath.

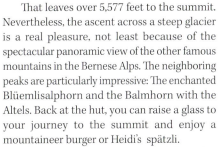

TOURS

TOUR 1 JEGERTOSSE
Doldenhornhütte → Fisialp, rocky trail to the Jegertosse
» 2,165 ft/660 m EG   » 2.4 mi/3.8 km
» 2.5 h   » easy

TOUR 2 DOLDENHORN
This route is not easy because it crosses glaciers and crevasses. However, the view from the top is great!
» 5,675 ft/1,730 m EG   » 2.9 mi/4.6 km
» 5.5 h   » medium

TOUR 3 OBERBÄRGLI
Round-trip trail on the N shore of Lake Oeschinen, via the Hohtürli and Oberbärgli.
» 1,575 ft/480 m EG   » 5.2 mi/8.3 km
» 3 h   » medium

Through the waterfall, you can see the turquoise waters of Lake Oeschinen. Refreshment on the go!

SWITZERLAND | BERN

The Insider Tip

FRÜNDENHÜTTE Lake Oeschinen glistens turquoise and clear in the sun, surrounded by a spectacular world of peaks. It's no wonder that it's popular in the summer. However, if you want to go higher, this idyllic mountain lake is just a stopover where you can recharge your batteries before continuing on to the Fründenhütte. Best of all: Once at the top, you'll have a most magnificent view of Lake Oeschinen.

Its location is surely the main reason many people hike to the Fründenhütte. Of course, it's possible to argue that most Alpine huts offer a spectacular view. Nevertheless, when you arrive, you'll want to sit in front of the hut first and not go in right away—just to enjoy the view. The Fründenhütte is framed by three peaks, the Dündenhorn, the Blüemlisalphorn, and the Doldenhorn. And thanks to its rough stone construction and red-and-white shutters, it fits beautifully into its surroundings. In summer, red flowers bloom in the windows, the large wooden door stands open invitingly. This is all reason enough to visit the Fründenhütte. But the best reason is that the hut, in contrast to Lake Oeschinen itself, is not overcrowded in the summer. So you don't have to fight for the best place in the sun—definitely the spot directly below the glacier, a few feet in front of the hut—from there you can enjoy the soothing home-style cuisine of the Fründenhütte in peace, and the view of the sunset is not blocked by countless other hikers. The Fründenhütte is a

The Fründenhütte is located where the mountain idyll of Lake Oeschinen merges into an abruptly rugged high alpine world of rock and ice.

SWITZERLAND | BERN | FRÜNDENHÜTTE

IN BRIEF

VALLEY TOWN Kandersteg

ALTITUDE 8,405 ft/2,562 m above sea level

OPEN June to September

ACCOMMODATIONS 58 beds in dormitories, winter room with 16 beds

FOOD Simple, but hearty and tasty meals for breakfast and dinner; hiking tea with half board.

GOOD TO KNOW Four-legged friends can stay in the wooden shed for free with prior registration—however, only one per night and only Sunday to Friday, reservations via online reservation system.

good insider tip. This is probably also due to the ascent, which is not easy. Although there is an easier path directly from the mountain lake to the hut, it's closed due to a threat of landslide. Therefore, there's no way to get to the hut except via the so-called "Frundenschnur." The trail is called the "Fründenschnur" ("friends' string") because it's actually as narrow as a string in places. A narrow band of grass runs directly along the rock face; on one side it drops off steeply, on the other it goes straight up. Surefootedness is definitely required here. You can't be afraid of heights if you're taking this path. This T4 route is secured with steel cables. For your trouble, you may encounter ibex and weasels, and if you're lucky, you'll also spot a golden eagle or a bearded vulture. However, you won't climb the path as elegantly as the ibex—you'll be happier once you've conquered the most exposed sections of the route and finally reach the Fründenhütte.

Your efforts will be rewarded by the warm hospitality of Marianne and Bernhard Winkler, who manage the hut and give every guest the feeling of coming home. The family-like atmosphere can easily hide the fact that life in a mountain hut is not always a bowl of cherries. There are no natural water sources left since

This goat seems to like Lake Oeschinen. (left) The red flowers in the cabin's windows create a cozy ambiance. (below)

FRÜNDENHÜTTE | BERN | SCHWEIZ

the glacier—which once encircled the entire hut—has receded more and more. Snow has to be melted or water from glacial lakes boiled for every cup of tea and delicious meal.

Solar panels and a diesel generator supply electricity. The ironclad rule of the hut's hosts is to use a maximum of 2.5 dl of diesel per guest, because people who live so close to nature worthy of protection do their best to preserve it and operate the hut as sustainably as possible. This also includes attention to food handling. Ingredients are flown in by helicopter, the food is freshly prepared, and no food is wasted. There are no showers at the Fründenhütte—if you want, you can take a refreshing dip in Lake Oeschinen on your way down.

Lake Oeschinen glistens, nestled between mighty rock faces; it's the most beautiful mountain lake in the Alps according to the Kandersteger. Its rich turquoise blue color is a unique natural spectacle.

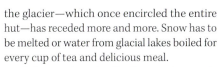

TOURS

TOUR 1 HEUBERG PANORAMA TRAIL
This round-trip hike starts at the Oeschinen mountain station, accessible from Kandersteg by gondola. With a view of Lake Oeschinen, it's the most beautiful panoramic hike in the Bernese Oberland.
» 3,478 ft/1,060 m EG » 6.8 mi/11 km
» 4.5 h » medium

TOUR 2 DOLDENHORN
You'll climb ice, snow, rock, and a spectacular firn ridge using fixed ropes, safety bars, and a rope ladder.
» 3,609 ft/1,100 m EG » 9 h » difficult

TOUR 3 FRÜNDENHORN
From the Fründenhütte on the NW ridge across the Fründen Glacier. Route includes a glacier crossing, many rock passages, a few short climbing spots, and an impressive firn ridge.
» 2,723 ft/830 m EG » 5 h » difficult

53

SWITZERLAND | BERN | FRÜNDENHÜTTE

Hut heroes

There are numerous stories about Marianne and Bernhard's outstanding hospitality. For example, one time, a female hiker ran out of breath and couldn't make the last few hundred feet to the hut. Her boyfriend ran ahead to see how far it was—and, to her great amazement, came back with a cup of bouillon that Marianne whipped up for her. Needless to say, she conquered the last stretch of the route thanks to this thoughtful refreshment. Bernhard performed another heroic feat when he "repaired" a hiker's boots with cable ties after the soles had come off completely; people say that this hiker walked all the way to Zürich.

A smart idea: Instead of leaving worn-out hiking boots on the mountain and walking back into the valley barefoot, cable ties kept the broken sole on the shoe.

FRÜNDENHÜTTE | BERN | SWITZERLAND

SWITZERLAND | BERN

The Wine Hut

BLÜEMLISALPHÜTTE The Blüemlisalphütte is a popular hut in the Bernese Alps. It is located on well-known hiking routes such as the Bärentrek, and it's the base for the demanding high-altitude tour of the Blüemlisalphorn. The hut's wine is truly special. Merlot, Syrah, and Pinot Noir from a small winery in the Valais mature in oak barrels in the cellar for three years.

The Blüemlisalphütte is a typical Swiss mountain hut. It's simple but cozy. There are no showers, just cold water for washing. There isn't any drinking water either. On arrival, hikers are divided among the dormitories—high-altitude hikers sleep in different rooms, and breakfast is served at different times.

It's evident that the hut is at an altitude of about 9,842 feet due to the increasingly thin air—both when hiking and sleeping, the latter of which works perfectly in most cases because of the duvets. They are incredibly warm and comfortable. And maybe it's also due to the delicious wine, which makes evenings in the hut convivial.

The Wuilloud family, which owns a small winery, and the former hut hosts Hildi and Hans have been friends for a long time. And that's why oak barrels full of delicious red wine from the Cave des Bouquetins Grimisuat Wallis winery are stored in the cellar of the Blümlisalp hut. It matures there for three years before hut guests can sample it.

← If you visit the Blüemlisalphütte, you should definitely plan an overnight stay, because then you can sit in front of the hut in the evening and enjoy the sunset.

SWITZERLAND | BERN | BLÜEMLISALPHÜTTE

The Blüemlisalphütte can accommodate 115 guests. Hut sleeping bags must either be brought along or purchased or borrowed in the hut. Breakfast is a buffet, which allows you to "tank up" for the day tour. Bread with butter, cheese, and jam are also included, and there's muesli too. Beverages are coffee, tea, cocoa, or milk. Once you have thoroughly explored the area and come back at lunchtime, you can choose between cold refreshments such as sandwiches, dried meat plates, and sliced cheese, or you can enjoy warm dishes such as rösti, soup, or spätzli. Dinner consists of three courses. First comes salad, vegetables, or a soup. Then the kitchen team conjures up a good main course, and at the end there is something delicious for dessert. If specified when you register, you can also enjoy a vegetarian menu. The box lunches are a great service. Just order the night before and take them with you in the morning. Hiking

IN BRIEF

VALLEY TOWN Kandersteg

ALTITUDE 9,318 ft/2,840 m above sea level

OPEN mid-June to mid-September

ACCOMMODATIONS 115 beds in dormitories, winter room with 10 beds

FOOD delicious homemade food, hot and cold drinks

GOOD TO KNOW Definitely take your time for the ascent. The unforgettable sunsets make the ascent worthwhile! No drinking water is available. Vegetarian menu if you pre-order.

BLÜEMLISALPHÜTTE | BERN | SWITZERLAND

The Hohtürli is a good hiking destination from the Blüemlisalphütte. The Wildstrubel and the Diablerets rise to the sky in the background.

You can see the hut from far away. Behind it, the Wildi Frau is the next summit.

tea that you can put in your own bottle is even included in the half board. Apart from the food, the Blüemlisalphütte's team is very experienced and they are passionate about hospitality.

In winter, there are 18 beds available in the hut. Woolen blankets are available, as is wood, which can be used to prepare a meal on the wood-burning stove. For this, however, you have to bring food and drinks with you. There is also no running water in the hut in the winter.

TOURS

TOUR 1 BÄRENTREK
Long-distance hike around the Bluemlisalp. Done in stages from Meiringen to Gsteig.
» 77,428 ft/23,600 m EG » 20 days
» 5 h » medium

TOUR 2 TO THE FRÜNDENHÜTTE
Around Lake Oeschinen or via the "Frundenschnur" → Frundenhutte → only for experienced hikers!
» 3,314 ft/1,010 m EG » 7.1 m/11.5 km
» 5 h » medium

TOUR 3 WILDLI FRAU
Half-day tour to the summit; requires a short 3rd degree climb.
» 1,476 ft/450 m EG » 0.8 mi/1.3 km
» 2.5 h » medium

🇨🇭 SWITZERLAND | BERN | BLÜEMLISALPHÜTTE

The legend of the Blüemlisalp

Once upon a time, the Blüemlisalp was a green, lush alpine pasture, where a young dairyman lived with his animals and servants. The dairyman became richer and richer, and soon he decided to marry. However, his wife wanted to be something special, which is why he washed her feet with milk every day and laid cheese wheels across the floor so that she didn't have to walk on the stones. His mother climbed to the alp to dissuade him from doing all this. When she arrived at the top, she was thirsty. The couple served her spoiled and dirty milk, which made the mother very angry. As punishment, she cursed the alp. Ice should cover the mountain and bury the couple and their animals. The mother set off on her descent, and suddenly, rock and ice fell from the sky and covered the Blüemlisalp, where it has been cold and icy ever since.

Whether you believe the legend or not is up to you. However, the fact is that the best milk for drinking—not for washing—comes from the Blüemlisalp.

BLÜEMLISALPHÜTTE | BERN | SWITZERLAND

SWITZERLAND | VALAIS

The High Alpine

Even in summer, the Mischabelhütte is surrounded by snow. It's a beautiful picture, especially when the sky is bright blue.

MISCHABELHÜTTE Anyone who ventures up here has a view of high alpine peaks—and has worked hard to get here. The ascent to the hut is difficult and therefore reserved for experienced mountaineers. The Mischabelhütte, at an altitude of 10,826 feet, presides over a stunning mountain panorama in the Swiss Valais. And a second building has been there since 1973.

If you look only at the subsurface on which the two multi-story wooden huts were built, you'll find yourself asking the question: "How in the world could people ever build here?" The jagged rocky ridge drops off on three sides, separating the Hohbalm Glacier from the Fall Glacier. Going uphill, toward the NE ridge to the Lenzspitze, the rock rises steeply right away. This is an extremely exposed location that an eagle might select for its aerie. The 360° view is long and phenomenal: With the Täschhorn, Dom, Lenzspitze, Nadelhorn, and Ulrichshorn—all over 13,123 feet high—the Mischabel Group provides majestic and fantastically beautiful summit scenery.

The fact the Mischabelhütte has made a perfect base for high mountain tours in the region for over 100 years is thanks to the Academic Alpine Club Zürich. It still owns the hut. Its members collected the money to carry building materials up the mountain on mule back starting in 1902; they built their own clubhouse on the Nadelgrat. The main building still stands, now renovated and modernized. Below that,

SWITZERLAND | VALAIS | MISCHABELHÜTTE

IN BRIEF

TVALLEY TOWN Saas Fee

ALTITUDE 10,958 ft/3,340 m above sea level

OPEN mid-June to mid-September

ACCOMMODATIONS 130 beds in dormitories, winter room with 40 beds

FOOD Dinner, breakfast, drinks, hiking tea, and a small daily menu with regional specialties

GOOD TO KNOW The cable car to Hannig cuts 1 hour off the ascent

Above Saas Fee, the path to the Mischabelhütte also leads across a narrow ladder. Surefootedness and sturdy shoes are therefore absolutely necessary.

there is a second hut, which goes back to the "Lange Wurst" project. In the 1970s, the original hut was bursting at the seams. One night, the hut's host counted 110 overnight guests, which was twice the hut's actual capacity. More space was needed. Plans were made to extend the hut lengthwise, that is, to turn it into a "long sausage." But because that would have created only 13 additional beds, they decided to blow the hut up in order to create a rock plateau for today's outbuilding.

Maria Anthamatten has managed the Mischabelhütte since 2011. She spent her first season on a construction site, because by outfitting the hut with roof water collection, storage tanks, and dry toilets, the Academic Alpine Club ensured the continued operation of the hut for the future. Climate change does not stop at the Valais either. The lack of water due to the receding glaciers causes problems for the Mischabelhütte.

At the same time, the power supply was renovated, solar panels installed, and the kitchen infrastructure modernized. This time, helicop-

MISCHABELHÜTTE | VALAIS | SWITZERLAND

ters rather than mules brought the material to this rough terrain.

You can see how exhausting the climb is from the faces of incoming climbers. After about four hours uphill from the valley, they reach the hut via ladders, pegs, and wire ropes. But all efforts are worthwhile as soon as you stretch out on the lovely sun terrace. In bad weather, the cozy interior entices, where hikers can relax quite well in the bright, lovingly decorated wooden lounge. The food is good, and if you have a birthday, you can get a piece of cake with a small birthday candle from the hut's crew—for mountain climbing isn't only about reaching peaks. ❄

TOURS

TOUR 1 NADELHORN
Complete with ice and crevasses: Ulrichshorn → Nadelhorn
» 3,494 ft/1,065 m EG » 4.1 mi/6.6 km
» 5.5 h » medium

TOUR 2 FROM THE BORDIERHÜTTE TO THE MISCHABELHÜTTE
Groß Bigerhorn & Ulrichshorn → Mischabelhutte; great view of the Lenzspitze
» 4,134 ft/1,260 m EG » 7.6 km
» 9 h » medium

TOUR 3 LENZSPITZE & NADELHORN
Challenging climb on NNE wall of the Lenzspitze Around the Nadelhorn, back on the normal trail.
» 4,206 ft/1,282 m EG » 8.2 mi/13.2 km
» 9 h » difficult

It's a sublime feeling when you finally reach the summit cross after the strenuous ascent, as here on the icy Nadelhorn.

65

🇨🇭 SWITZERLAND | VALAIS | MISCHABELHÜTTE

Curiosities of the Mischabelhütte

Once the flag is raised at the hut and the season is open, news of strange animal observations travels down to the valley. The extremely rare mountain gull has already been spotted in various places around the Mischabelhütte. In the past, even polar bears and pink rabbits are said to have strayed to the high altitude. Photos prove it … they're publicly available on social media. It's now clear that the hut is characterized by a pleasant mixture of joy in sporting performance, awe for the beauty of nature, and plenty of joie de vivre. A barrel of ice becomes the ultimate plunge pool and the cleared terrace an e-bike parcours. The motto is always: "If not now, when?"

→

You can decide for yourself whether a hut guest really saw a pink rabbit at the Mischabelhütte. Perhaps it was just an optical illusion caused by the heather.

MISCHABELHÜTTE | VALAIS | SWITZERLAND

SWITZERLAND | BERN

10

The Comfortable One

When leaving the Gaulihütte, the three young women have a fabulous view of the Gauli Glacier.

GAULIHÜTTE The Gaulihütte's buildings stand next to each other like brothers in a family photo: The "old Hüttli", the veteran, and the younger one, small and full of energy. They are surrounded by forget-me-nots, wild orchid, and gentian. Even the rare alpine anemones can be found here. It isn't their delicate yellow flowers that make the hut unique, but rather the numerous stories that people tell about it.

Even the construction of the Gaulihütte involves a special story. In 1894, an Englishman fell in love with the Alpine panorama and especially with the Gauli region with its numerous glaciers and lakes. Carl Ludwig Lory, the Englishman, finally decided to build a hut in this beautiful landscape, and the farming community even donated land for it. About 10,500 kg of material had to be towed up the mountain to build the hut—and nobody envied the porters, who often needed more than four hours for the ascent. The Gaulihütte was dedicated one year later, in 1895. But Lory did not want the hut just for himself, so he decided to give it to the Swiss Alpine Club.

A lot has changed since then. The building was expanded, a solar system built, and even the environment has changed due to the retreat of the glaciers. However, some things have remained the same, namely the hut's quaint atmosphere and authentic feeling that visitors enjoy. This means that there's no wifi, but great

69

human companionship; no bubbling water pipe, but tea from boiled glacier water; a strenuous ascent, but then chamois milk or beer as a reward; and much more. Hut hosts Katrin and Roger will provide "Glutschtigs" (tasty treats) from the kitchen, ranging from hearty rösti to delicious cakes. In the evening, there is even a three-course menu for hikers.

Afterwards, life is cozy in the Gaulihütte. You can sit on the wood bench by the stove with its red-and-white-checkered cushions and talk to friends old and new about the most beautiful moments on the ascent, or listen to tales about the "Gauliweiblein" (a local wandering spirit) and a spectacular rescue operation in 1946. Or you can put the Jass cards on the table, then the mood is cheerful to the point of rambunctiousness, and laughter fills the simply yet comfortably furnished room. You can recharge your batteries for the next day with a quiet night in one of the four rooms, which offer a total of 60 beds. And in the morning, the hiking tea is ready and waiting. While you warm yourself up, you can survey the awakening Urbachtal, which is often filled with low-hanging clouds in the morning.

Those who do not want to start their descent right away will find excellent climbing opportunities on the gneiss and varied hiking trails nearby. Its remote location makes the Gaulihütte an ideal starting point for intensive nature experiences.

However, the location is also a challenge for the hut's hosts. Food is flown in by helicopter, and the quietest place is the composting toilet. By the way, you can visit the Gaulihütte in winter too. It is not hosted from mid-October to February, but the "old Hüttli" is available as a

A high-contrast backdrop: On one side of Lake Gauli is the Gauli Glacier; on the other side, the mountain meadow features colorful flowers.

IN BRIEF

VALLEY TOWN Innertkirchen

ALTITUDE 7,234 ft/2,205 m above sea level

OPEN March to May; July to mid-October; shelter open year round

ACCOMMODATIONS 65 beds, heated winter room

FOOD Hiking tea in the AM; hearty dishes such as rösti, soup, cheese, and sausage later; 3-course menu in the evening; box lunches on request

GOOD TO KNOW Climbing rocks, waterfalls, and even an airplane wreck are nearby.

GAULIHÜTTE | BERN | SWITZERLAND

The use of space in the Gaulihütte is exemplary: Guests even sleep in the attic.

shelter during this period. Trapped entirely in a white winter wonderland, the Gauli region has its charms in winter. The hard-boiled hikers who are on the road then are usually adventurous enough not to yearn for luxury accommodation but are looking for exactly what the Gaulihütte is all about in winter: Cooking on the wood stove, no running water. The dormitory accommodates 21 guests.

TOURS

TOUR 1 WATERFALL TRAIL
The impressive "Waterfall Trail" runs from Innertkirchen → Gaulihütte; nice mini via ferrata.
» 6,168 ft/1,880 m EG   » 18.6 mi/30 km
» 11 h   » difficult

TOUR 2 EWIGSCHNEEHORN
High-altitude ski tour with glacier ascent; Gaulipass and great views of 4000m peaks.
» 3,937 ft/1,200 m EG   » 3.7 mi/6 km
» 5 h   » medium

TOUR 3 HANGENDGLETSCHERHORN
The view from the Gaulihütte is gorgeous. The trail over the Chammligrat includes a climbing passage.
» 3,609 ft/1,100 m EG   » 6.2 mi/10 km
» 6 h   » difficult

SWITZERLAND | BERN | GAULIHÜTTE

Dakota C-53

The name "Gauli" will ring a bell for anyone familiar with the history of Swiss air rescue. The Gauli Glacier was the focus of worldwide attention in 1946 due to a near-tragedy that, fortunately, had a cinematic happy ending. It is regarded as the birth of the Swiss air rescue service. In November, an American Dakota C-53 crashed on the glacier during a flight over the Alps. The subsequent rescue operation lasted six days and was a pioneering achievement: Never before had an air rescue been attempted on high alpine terrain. So it's all the more gratifying that this idea, born of necessity, saved the lives of the twelve passengers. The Gaulihütte is still part of this story, and there are even tours to the crash site from the hut.

Happiness in misfortune: The twelve people on the American Dakota that crashed on the Gauli Glacier in November 1946 were rescued successfully.

GAULIHÜTTE | BERN | SWITZERLAND

73

SWITZERLAND | TICINO

The Spaceship

CAPANNA CORNO GRIES If you are looking for an alpine hut with dark wooden beams and a low roof or a farmhouse with colorful shutters, you shouldn't head for the Corno Gries. However, if you'd like to evoke astonished reactions to your tour photos, you should definitely go there. "Where have you been?" might be the question—and the answer: In Ticino! "Although it looks like the moon."

A barren landscape surrounds the Capanna Corno Gries. Slate interspersed with garnet inclusions is typical. There are no trees at this height, only a little mossy grass growing here and there on the rugged peaks. Glaciers sparkle in the sun, competing with Lake Gries, the turquoise lake at the foot of the Gries Glacier, which feeds it. Amidst of this scenery, about 1.9 miles from Lake Gries as the crow flies, the extraordinary building of the Capanna Corno Gries presides over the Val Corno.

It was built in the 1920s, but it has been extended and renovated since then and so assumed its present appearance gradually. Probably the most striking construction was done in 2007 by the architect Silvano Caccia. He transformed an "ordinary" mountain hut into a modern building, which was rightfully nicknamed "the spaceship." During the renovation, the hut's roof was removed and an all-glass story was added, then a wood structure was placed on top; at first, it looks like an inverted roof. In the midst of the barren lunar landscape, the hut looks po-

← Its appearance makes the Capanna Corno Gries unmistakable. It rises futuristically from the classic mountain landscape of peaks and flowery meadows.

SWITZERLAND | TICINO | CAPANNA CORNO GRIES

IN BRIEF

VALLEY TOWN All'Acqua (Bedretto)

ALTITUDE 7,670 ft/2,338 m above sea level

OPEN March to April; mid-June to early/mid-October; winter room year round.

ACCOMMODATIONS 46 beds in 8 dormitories, winter room with 40 beds

FOOD large breakfast, during the day hot and cold dishes and cake, everything is prepared at the hut.

GOOD TO KNOW Children are definitely welcome in the Capanna Corno Gries! You can also bring your four-legged friends if you register them in advance.

Sitting on a stone and letting the scenery wash over you is a "must" on a hike through the region around the Corno Gries.

sitively extraterrestrial, but there's a practical reason for its shape, for the three-part division is reflected inside the hut as well. The dining room and lounge are on the middle floor. Thanks to the surrounding glass wall, there is a wonderful 360° panoramic view from here—ideal for those who couldn't get enough of the impressive landscape on the border between Swiss Ticino and Italian Piedmont on the way to the hut.

But even the most beautiful day will eventually come to an end. And when the last ray of sunshine has finally disappeared behind the peaks of the Gotthard massif, the hikers go up a floor. Here, in the wooden "roof on your head," there are eight rooms that house overnight guests. While it's sad that you have to leave the view of the mountain panorama, at least you won't be sad after you've climbed into the comfortable beds. Then your body can finally recover from the strenuous hike, and images of the barren environment will float through your dreams.

But when you look at the menu, you'll see that the name "Alpine spaceship" isn't entirely accurate because you'll soon see that the food has nothing to do with the unappetizing freeze-

CAPANNA CORNO GRIES | TICINO | SWITZERLAND

dried rations packed for astronauts. Regional and seasonal specialties and organic products are highlighted in the the Capanna Corno Gries. And the hosts know that everything tastes best when it's homemade, which is why everything is freshly prepared in the hut. After a restful sleep, you start the next day with bread made from organic grain milled in-house and honey or the best alpine cheese. During the day, you can fortify yourself with cold sandwiches, gnocchi, or polenta. Food and this unique location tempt us not to think about the descent but rather to stay longer in the "spaceship." However, even Alpine astronauts have to go home someday. ❄

TOURS

TOUR 1 BLINNENHORN
Across the Corno, Gries, and Rothorn passes to the Blinnenhorn; treacherous glacial landscape.
» 3,576 ft/1,090 m EG   » 7.5 mi/12 km
» 6.5 h   » medium

TOUR 2 FOUR-SPRINGS-TRAIL
Explore the Gotthard massif in 5 stages; trail runs past the Capanna Corno Gries. Or hike part of the trail.
» 13,648 ft/4,160 m EG   » 49.7 mi/80 km
» 29 h   » medium

TOUR 3 GRIESHORN
The trail around the Kleine Grieshorn to the Grieshorn is not long, but scree fields require experience.
» 2,461 ft/750 m EG   » 2.5 mi/4 km
» 2 h   » difficult

It's not just hikers who appreciate the area and the Nufenen Pass. Along the way, they meet cuddly Valais black-nosed sheep.

SWITZERLAND | TICINO | CAPANNA CORNO GRIES

The Capanna's secret recipe

If you return home and rave about the delicious food, you can recreate some at home. The Capanna Corno Gries has revealed its recipe for "Il tortino al cioccolato fondente," seductive dark chocolate torte:

Beat two eggs and 50 g of sugar until creamy. Melt 100 g of butter and 100 g of dark chocolate in a double boiler and then mix with 30 g of flour. Add everything to the egg and sugar mixture. Now pour into five small tins sprinkled with cocoa and refrigerate for five hours. Then bake at 410° F for seven minutes in the preheated oven, let cool for two minutes, and turn onto plates.

These dreamy tortes are served in the hut with ice cream or fresh berries.

Fresh berries and ice cream are the "icing on the cake" of these delicious chocolate tortes, which are homemade at the Capanna Corno Gries.

CAPANNA CORNO GRIES | TICINO | SWITZERLAND

SWITZERLAND | URI

12

The Children's Paradise

Right next to the Sewenhütte, there is a so-called Tyrolienne, where children can ride a zip line across meadows and a narrow rift.

SEWENHÜTTE Dwarves' trail, blueberries, a lake for swimming, climbing gardens, and an airy zip line. The Sewenhütte in the Uri Alps has become a true paradise for children and families. It's therefore not surprising that climbers and high-altitude hikers share the hut with families or even entire school classes.

We have our heavy climbing and high-altitude backpacks with us as we come up the trail. We want to spend several days at the Sewenhütte in the Uri Alps. And just a few minutes after our arrival, we are charmed by the hut hosts' warm welcome and the delicious welcome drink.

We quickly realize that we're the exception up here. As part of a school trip, there are several classes at the Sewenhütte, so it's very lively during our stay. Right near the hut, there are several climbing walls and climbing gardens where the children can really let off steam. Nearby Lake Sewen offers an opportunity to cool down and splash, even if the water is a bit cold. You can go for a paddle on the lake. A special highlight is the zip line in front of the hut, so it's not surprising that there are lots of children here. But the SAC section Pfannenstiel's charming, cozy, authentic Swiss mountain hut is definitely worth a visit for young and old.

A warm shower provides a certain comfort, even if showers should be kept short due to the lack of water in the mountains. A wood stove and solar system heat the water.

SWITZERLAND | URI | SEWENHÜTTE

And the food is important too. Simple and delicious dishes include the hearty Sewenplättli, the Meiental potato casserole, and sweet Älplermagronen, which are served with applesauce. The little ones are especially excited about the breakfast with cornflakes and chocolate spread from the ample XXL jar.

There's a lot to do around the hut, especially for climbing enthusiasts. You decide: a relatively simple climb on the Sewenkegel, a steep tour on the Sewenhorn-Westgratturm or a seemingly never-ending climb on the Hochsewen-Südgrat.

There's also an ideal warm-up tour for high-altitude hikers on the Bächenstock. You can climb a 9842-foot peak for the first time here. If you don't want to do that, you can climb the Spitzplangstock. Although this hike is a T3/T4, it can be done with more experienced children and appropriate caution.

Only when descending from the hut do we notice the many blueberries along the trail.

IN BRIEF

VALLEY TOWN Gorezmettlenbach

ALTITUDE 7,047 ft/2,148 m above sea level

OPEN early June to mid-October, some years even at Easter

ACCOMMODATIONS 60 beds (family rooms too), heated winter room

FOOD Simple menu featuring regional dishes.

GOOD TO KNOW Bring swimsuit, climbing and high-altitude equipment.

SEWENHÜTTE | URI | SWITZERLAND

Right near the hut, there are several climbing gardens of various degrees of difficulty. Some climbing supplies can be borrowed.

Our backpacks were probably too heavy on the ascent to pay close attention to the natural landscape. The delicious berries make children very happy; be sure to leave time for berry-picking. Just as exciting for children is the dwarves' trail set up on the ascent to the hut. All these ingredients make the Sewenhütte one of the best family and children's huts in Switzerland, ideal for your first mountain adventures on rock and ice.

TOURS

TOUR 1 DWARVES' TRAIL
Gorezmettlen → mountain forest → dwarf-themed trail
» 2,034 ft/620 m EG   » 3.7 mi/6 km
» 2.5 h   » easy

TOUR 2 SUSTLIHÜTTE
This trail leads past the steep walls of the Chli Spannort.
» 1,968 ft/600 m EG   » 4.0 mi/6.5 km
» 4 h   » medium

TOUR 3 GURTNELLEN VILLAGE
Winds over the Rot Bergli, down into the lonely Gornerental, ends in Gurtnellen.
» 1,050 ft/320 m EG   » 8.1 mi/13 km
» 5 h   » difficult

The concept of the hut's hosts, Ursi and Walter, works well: If the children are happy, so are the parents.

HUT BOOK

HUT BOOK

Huts all over

The broader view: Spectacular huts in the mountains of the world, from the Andes to New Zealand

After the exploration of the Alps, the first huts and shelters were built in mountains outside of Europe. Some spectacular specimens are worth discovering. The oldest hut in Mount Cook National Park in New Zealand is the Sefton Bivvy, which offers space for climbers and glacier hikers to sleep in four small berths. Many other well-known mountains around the world also feature impressive shelters: On the Chimborazo, the Edward Whymper Refuge, named after the legendary first person to ascend the Matterhorn, is at more than 16,400 feet. The Piedra Grande hut is the base for the Pico di Orizaba in Mexico, and the Toubkal hut is considered the base camp for trekking tours in the High Atlas in Morocco. On the famous Mt. Fuji in Japan, there are 40 huts for ascending the holy volcano.

For generations, the Sefton Bivvy beneath Mount Footstool has been providing beds for four people.

85

SWITZERLAND | GRAUBÜNDEN

The Perfect One

TERRIHÜTTE The surroundings: A dream. The hut: ditto. The Greina plateau promises pure wilderness, which is not unjustly compared to northern Sweden or North American national parks. And this is where the Terrihütte awaits its guests. It offers comfortable beds for more than 100 hikers. Toni, the hut host, gives everyone his best and knows how to perfect hikers' stays with advice and delicious food.

Depending on the route you choose, the hike to the Terrihütte can really make you sweat. This means you'll be really glad to reach the hut. Then it's time to swap your sturdy hiking boots for the sandals you have brought along and wiggle all ten toes until they feel completely free and comfortable again. Once you've done this, you can relax on the terrace and quench your thirst with a radler or apple juice spritzer. You'll certainly get to know some like-minded people, soon enough, you'll be trading reports about today's hike—some people may even tell of an encounter with a cuddly marmot—and share the last rest of your trail provisions with one another. Or did you eat everything on the march to the hut? No problem! You can recharge with the homemade nut cake or legendary Greina cake. However, with all the eating and talking, you shouldn't forget to take a good look around you. because the view is the main reason why you shouldn't go inside right away. Instead, take a seat on the terrace as long as the weather permits. From here you can look down into the Val

← When the fog slowly creeps over the peaks, you should take the last steps to the Terrihütte a little faster–not just because dinner is waiting.

87

SWITZERLAND | GRAUBÜNDEN | TERRIHÜTTE

IN BRIEF

VALLEY TOWN Sumvitg

ALTITUDE 7,119 ft/2,170 m above sea level

OPEN mid-June to mid-October

ACCOMMODATIONS 110 in 12 dormitory rooms, 22 beds in the winter room

FOOD classic breakfast, 3-course dinner, and sweet treats from the bakery during the day, box lunches on request

GOOD TO KNOW Bring a hut sleeping bag. There are no showers in the Terrihütte.

Of course, a herd of cows is part of the idyllic landscape of the Greina plain; the cows are probably happier about the lush grass than about the panoramic view here.

Sumvitg and up to the Tödi. And even the most experienced hikers won't be able to get enough of this panorama.

Seeing a lot is one thing, eating a lot's the other—and fortunately the latter is not a problem thanks to the excellent hospitality. Dinner is served starting at 7:00 PM. It consists of soup, salad, a tasty main course, and dessert. After dinner, you can take out the playing cards or talk to other guests some more. The hut hosts Doris and Toni are also happy to tell stories or help you plan the rest of your route. By the way, the hut also offers its guests a glass of wine in the evening—a luxury that you usually don't get in huts.

At some point, however, you should go to bed, because for most people, a challenging hike is on the agenda the next day. People who wear glasses will notice that there is no shelf space directly next to the beds, so it's best to put your glasses in your backpack before snuggling under the warm blanket.

The next morning in the Terrihütte begins with a classic breakfast, consisting of bread baked fresh in the hut, with cheese, jam, and butter. You can also have muesli, and there is plenty of fresh coffee to get you going. Anyone who ordered a box lunch the day before will pack up

88

TERRIHÜTTE | GRAUBÜNDEN | SWITZERLAND

their sandwiches, and far too soon they will say goodbye to this special place.

In winter, when the Terrihütte is not hosted, hikers have a shelter with 22 beds. Then a stay is a special experience. It's a big adventure after a winter hike when you unpack your food in an unattended hut and you're all alone in the snowy mountains.

TOURS

TOUR 1 PIZ VIAL
Across the Greina plain, then hike and climb to the summit of Piz Vial via the W Ridge. The descent leads down the S flank. Take a ski tour in good snow conditions.
» 3,444 ft/1,050 m EG » 4.0 mi/6.4 km
» 4 h » medium

TOUR 2 LAGO DI LUZZONE
W across the Greina plain on the Muot la Greina past the Crap la Crusch. Stop at at Campanna Motterascio.
» 1,214 ft/370 m EG » 8.5 mi/13.6 km
» 5 h » easy

TOUR 3 KRONENWANDERUNG
9th stage of the Kronenwanderung: go via Fuorcla Sura da Lavaz and small glaciers to the Medelserhütte at an altitude of 2,524 m.
» 3,182 ft/970 m EG » 7.4 mi/12 km
» 5 h » difficult

Rushing loudly, the waterfall announces itself before you see it. The view is particularly beautiful when the alpine vegetation is in bloom all around.

SWITZERLAND | GRAUBÜNDEN | TERRIHÜTTE

Bivouac in the hut

When a wholesale renovation of the Terrihütte was required in 2007, the hut maintenance team hired the architect Gion A. Caminada. The aim was to make hikers' stay a very special one and make the Terrihütte a little more perfect. And finally they had this brilliant idea: Instead of putting all the beds in the large dormitories typical of mountain huts, walls were moved in to create individual rooms that would accommodate four or more beds. But that's not all. Another innovative idea was also implemented. In the basement of the newer part of the building, so-called "bivouac rooms" were set up, whose sleeping berths, thanks to partitions and windows that open to the outside, remind people of camping!

The lights come on early in the Terrihütte, regardless of whether the guests slept well or "bivouacked" in this hut's innovative rooms.

TERRIHÜTTE | GRAUBÜNDEN | SWITZERLAND

SWITZERLAND | APPENZELL

14

The Nostalgic One

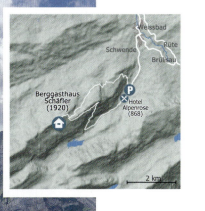

BERGGASTHAUS SCHÄFLER The Alpstein is a small, fine, wild mountain range in the eastern Swiss Alps; the Schäfler is a smaller mountain in the northern part of this area. For more than 100 years, the Berggasthaus Schäfler has stood on its summit; with its nostalgic furnishings, it takes us back to the era when it was built.

We are sitting at the Berggasthaus Schäfler, warming ourselves in the wonderful fall sun. Although it's already early November, its rays are still astonishingly powerful. After this morning, that's just the ticket. It was bitterly cold in the parking lot in Wasserauen, which was unusually full for a weekday in November. But the many hikers quickly spread out on the most diverse trails. Just a few people like us chose the route over the alp and to the Schäfler.

When you finally arrive at the Berggasthaus, you will be captivated by its magic. There is a panoramic view of the Alpstein and the Appenzeller Land. You can imagine how magnificent a sunset must be up here.

It's a wonderful experience to stay overnight in the Berggasthaus Schäfler. In addition to the sunrise, there are nostalgic double rooms that haven't changed since the hut was built in 1914. There are no sinks in the rooms, but there are water jugs and wash basins, just as there were 100 years ago. The dormitory rooms, by contrast, have been modernized and exude precisely the coziness that you would expect in a real mountain hut. The hut's hosts will spoil you with

The summit location on the Schäfler provides a magnificent view. The wild landscape here in the Alpstein is breathtaking.

93

SWITZERLAND | APPENZELL | BERGGASTHAUS SCHÄFLER

delicious local dishes such as rösti and Siedwurst. The region's famous cheese, spicy Appenzell, is also on the menu. It's particularly nice that you can eat your hearty snack right on the terrace so that you can keep enjoying the impressive panorama while you're eating. And if the weather doesn't play along, it's also great to sit and dine in the very cozy Swiss-style room.

When Franz Döring built the hut, all the building materials had to be carried on muleback to the Schäfler. Fortunately, today mules no longer have to handle the transport. Thanks to the construction of a material cableway built in the 1960s, it's now much easier to get food and such. A few years later, electricity was added; it's now supplied by diesel emergency power generators.

We're somewhat surprised at how much is going on up here. After all, our climb was quite challenging. When descending, however, we realize how easy the trail from the mountain station of the cable car to the Ebenenalp is. It's

IN BRIEF

VALLEY TOWN Wasserauen

ALTITUDE 6,322 ft/1,920 m above sea level

OPEN June to September

ACCOMMODATIONS 15 beds in single or multi-bed rooms, 70-bed room

FOOD good Appenzell cuisine with local specialties

GOOD TO KNOW Ride the Ebenenalp cable car. Alternative requires sturdy shoes, surefootedness, and experience.

BERGGASTHAUS SCHÄFLER | APPENZELL | SWITZERLAND

At the Rotsteinpass, the bright colors of countless flowers adorn the path and invite you to stop and admire them.

easy to walk here in just an hour. It's a good way to enjoy the mountain experience at the Schäfler, even if it's not quite as impressive as our way. ❈

TOURS

TOUR 1 ÖHRLIKOPF
Not-too-difficult hike to the Ohrlikopf; good signs, steel ropes keep less experienced hikers safe in many places.
» 1,003 ft/306 m EG   » 1.9 mi/3.1 km
» 1.5 h   » easy

TOUR 2 ROUND-TRIP TRAIL WITH LAKE SEEALP
Round trip from the Schäfler → Wildkirchli, through watery meadows to Lake Seealp. Take a dip in the lake, then → Schäfler via the Altenalp.
» 3,789 ft/1,155 m EG   » 7.5 mi/12 km
» 7 h   » medium

The sometimes very narrow paths around the Schäfler are often equipped with ropes to keep hikers safe.

SWITZERLAND | APPENZELL | BERGGASTHAUS SCHÄFLER

A giant's home

The famous geologist Albert Heim once described the Alpstein in the Oststein as the most beautiful mountain range in the world. And that's not by chance: With its steep grass flanks and three deep blue mountain lakes, it's truly a jewel. So it's not surprising that the giant Säntis chose to live in this wonderful area. According to legend, when he was tired, he lay down in his bed, today's Schwendibachtal, where the green pastures of the Meglisalp served as his pillow. Lake Seealp formed where the giant leaned his elbow when he got up. The many lonely houses in the Appenzell region are said to have been built when a farmer cut a slit in the giant's booty sack, in which he had previously collected people's houses in order to play with them. The houses fell out of the slit and were scattered widely across the country. And after this incident, the giant was never seen again.

The legend about the giant Säntis, who also gave the famous summit its name, is not really necessary; the landscape itself is mystical enough.

BERGGASTHAUS SCHÄFLER | APPENZELL | SWITZERLAND

🇱🇮 LIECHTENSTEIN

Principality and trustee—these are probably the first words people associate with Liechtenstein. And there's something else that most people also know: Liechtenstein is relatively small. There are only five countries in the world that are smaller than Liechtenstein. Neglecting it in travel planning would not only be unfair, but it would also miss out on the beautiful landscape that this Alpine country has to offer. Of course, the number of mountain huts is not large, but with the Pfälzerhütte, the Liechtenstein Alpine Club has a hut that is just as suitable for a day hike as it is as a stage destination for multi-day hikes. For example, one route of the Via Alpina trail network passes by here. And after a hike in Liechtenstein, surely the list of words associated with the principality will include terms such as "idyll" and "panoramic views."

Some colorful flowers grow along the wayside, but otherwise green dominates in many parts of the fantastically beautiful Rätikon.

LIECHTENSTEIN | TRIESENBERG

15

The Only One

PFÄLZERHÜTTE In 1928, after nine sections of the German and Austrian Alpine Associations merged to form the Palatinate Alpine Association, they built a two-story stone building below the Naafkopf, and the small principality of Liechtenstein had its first mountain hut: the Pfälzerhütte.

The sun is shining, the snow is glittering, but unfortunately the Pfälzerhütte is closed today. That's no wonder; after all, it is March, and the hut only opens its doors in the summer. We still visited it briefly as part of a ski tour from Malbun across the Augstenberg. After a break, we will successfully conclude our tour, descending across untouched powder snow slopes through the beautiful Valünatal.

In the summer, hikers and mountain bikers cavort here; they stop for a bite to eat with the hospitable host René Keel, enjoying simple dishes such as Käsplättli (cheese plates), and relaxing in beautiful nature. René took over the hut from Elfriede Beck in 2020. The latter, a South Tyrolean, came to Liechtenstein at the age of 16, first worked in a café, learned the regional dialect, and then managed the Pfälzerhütte for many years.

The Palatinate Alpine Association was formed in 1928, and it decided to build a shelter in Liechtenstein's Alps on the border with Austria and Switzerland. This was the first, and at that time also the only, hut in the principality. During the Second World War, the shelter was loo-

The main stone building of the Pfälzerhütte and its outbuilding with the winter room, which is called the "Eagle," are surrounded by soft green.

LIECHTENSTEIN | TRIESENBERG | PFÄLZERHÜTTE

IN BRIEF

VALLEY TOWN Malbun

ALTITUDE 6,916 ft/2,108 m above sea level

OPEN mid-June to mid-October

ACCOMMODATIONS 11 beds, 51-bed dormitory, 20 emergency berths

FOOD simple dishes, mostly only one main course

GOOD TO KNOW Simple, cozy, small hut, 32x42 feet in the beautiful Bettlerjoch.

Many people aren't familiar with the Rätikon, but hiking there takes you through idyllic mountain landscapes that inevitably feature lots of cows.

ted and damaged several times, and it was eventually forgotten. It did not reopen until 1950. In 1963, the Palatinate Alpine Association was granted the right to purchase the hut, something it did only in 1980. Today, it is owned by the Liechtenstein Alpine Club, which takes loving care of it. The small shelter is still a cozy and authentic mountain hut that can only accommodate about 60 people. Somehow, this doesn't fit in at all with the large buildings in Liechtenstein's financial center. But that's fine with us; modesty suits the Pfälzerhütte well. After all, beautiful moments are priceless. And you will certainly experience beautiful moments here. For example, there's the view of the green meadows when you're sitting on the terrace.

Today, the Pfälzerhütte is no longer considered Liechtenstein's "only one." The Gafadurahütte, which also belongs to the Alpine Association, has joined it.

The hut's summit is next to the Augstenberg of the Naafkopf, which is at 8,431 feet. It stands right where Liechtenstein, Switzerland, and Austria meet. But the most exciting destinati-

PFÄLZERHÜTTE | TRIESENBERG | LIECHTENSTEIN

on is the Vordere Grauspitze, which at 8,526 feet is the highest mountain in Liechtenstein. It is thus one of the seven summits of the Alps, the highest peaks in those seven Alpine countries: Slovenia, Austria, Italy, Switzerland, France, Germany, and Liechtenstein. Despite its relatively low height, the summit must not be underestimated. The terrain is steep, sloping, and exposed.

The Pfälzerhütte displays its strengths as a base for a hiking tour lasting several days. On impressive trails, for example, you hike to the Mannheimer Hütte on the west side of the Schesaplana or to the Schesaplanahütte on the south side. The good Swiss and Liechtenstein bus network offers easy return options to Malbun, and thus plenty of opportunities for the imaginative hiker to string several hut experiences together. ✻

On the way to the summit, you can see why this high-altitude trail is simply called the "Panorama trail." When you finally reach the top, the view is magnificent.

TOURS

TOUR 1 VIA ALPINA–ROTER WEG
The Via Alpina runs through all the Alpine countries. The Roter Weg runs past the Pfälzerhütte. From here, hike the 59th stage → Schesaplana Hütte. Even though this isn't far, you'll cross two national borders. If that's not enough, you can hike the entire Roter Weg from Trieste → Monaco through all 8 Alpine countries.
» 1,158 ft/353 m EG   » 5.3 mi/8.6 km
» 3.5 h   » medium

TOUR 2 PANORAMAWEG
Delivers exactly what its name promises! The 1st stage of the Panoramaweg, no. 66 in the opposite direction, starts at the Pfälzerhütte, across the Augstenberg, via the Fürstin-Gina-Weg → Malbun.
» 935 ft/285 m EG   » 4.8 mi/7.7 km
» 3.5 h   » medium

103

 # GERMANY

The Chiemgau Alps, Ester Mountains, the Allgäu—Germany's south is characterized by incredibly beautiful mountain landscapes. They rise up as you approach from the north, moving from alpine upland to actual mountains. And finally you are surrounded by inspiring scenery with high peaks and green valleys, the air is filled with the sound of cowbells and the scent of freedom.

Of course, being out and about in the mountains is not always fun and games. Rainy weather, steep ascents, and missing signposts can make life difficult. So it's really nice to arrive at a hut that offers not only a restorative meal and a place to sleep, but also warm hospitality that makes all your troubles go away.

Beautiful views on the way to the Schrecksee in the Allgäu Alps. The small, magical health resort of Bad Hindelang in the Ostrachtal is visible in the background.

GERMANY | BAVARIA

16

The Modern One

WALTENBERGERHAUS The Waltenbergerhaus presides high above the Bacherloch. This bright wooden building lights the way for hikers—whether they are day hikers or hiking the Heilbronner Weg. The hut was rebuilt in 2016, a project that turned out to be a real feat due to its exposed location, so there is now a modern refuge on the Allgäu Hauptkamm.

It cannot be denied that there were disputes over the reconstruction of the hut. In particular, people feared that the coziness of this hut's predecessor would be lost. But in the process, people forgot that the hut was actually too small and there was no drying room. Especially in bad weather, the old hut quickly became uncomfortable.

Now such worries are a thing of the past. There has been a modern hut with state-of-the-art technology up here since 2016. Has the coziness really been lost? This may be a matter of opinion, but the spacious lounges still exude a homey flair. In the new building, planners worked to ensure that there would be as many seats in the dining room as there are beds. This way, the Waltenbergerhaus never gets too full, and every overnight guest can eat in peace. The sunny, south-facing terrace is a dream. Ibex often come here to visit in the mornings and evenings.

And the hut's power supply has also been modernized. There's a battery system and a hot water storage tank, in addition to the 100 solar panels

Thanks to its high alpine location, you can enjoy a magnificent view of the Allgäu Hauptkamm (main ridge) from the Waltenberghaus.

107

GERMANY | BAVARIA | WALTENBERGERHAUS

on the roof. The warm exhaust air from cooling units is used to heat the drying room. All of this enabled the hut to qualify for the Alpine Association's environmental seal of approval.

Rebuilding the hut required top-notch logistics. After all, everything had to be flown up the mountain, even the excavator and the crane. Construction required more than 2,000 helicopter flights. Markus Kärlinger and his wife Claudia continue to host the hut. They had everything under control in the old hut, and they still spoil their guests with delicious dishes. After the hike, you can enjoy traditional dishes such as liver dumpling soup and "Käsnudla" (cheese noodles) or unusual ones such as the spicy lentil dish Nepali Dal. Of course, the menu has to include some sweet treats: Kaiserschmarrn, apple strudel, and their like will make you drool.

The Waltenbergerhaus is popular as a base for the Heilbronner Weg, which actually runs

IN BRIEF

VALLEY TOWN Birgsau

ALTITUDE 6,840 ft/2,085 m above sea level

OPEN Pentecost to early October

ACCOMMODATIONS 42 beds in multi-bed rooms, 28-bed dormitory

FOOD hearty regional cuisine with breakfast, lunch, and dinner, or half board

GOOD TO KNOW The Heilbronner Weg is challenging and awesome. Ideally, hikers divide it across three days. Reservations only via online portal.

WALTENBERGERHAUS | BAVARIA | GERMANY

The former hamlet of Einödsbach, 3 houses and a chapel, enjoys a magnificent view of the Trettachspitze and the Mädelegabel.

Together with the Hochfrottspitze and the Trettachspitze, the Mädelegabel is part of the famous Allgäu Dreigestirn.

from the Rappenseehütte to the Kemptner Hütte. However, since the Heilbronner Weg is very long, many climbers hike from the Bockkarscharte through the Bockkar down to the Waltenbergerhaus and then spend the night there. The new building is especially important if you have paid a visit to the Mädelegabel first. When bad weather is on the way, there's no other reliable base in this area. So you can be glad that the Alpine Club decided to build a new building and put this modern hut up here. The authorities probably wouldn't have allowed the old hut to keep operating much longer anyway.

TOURS

TOUR 1 TRETTACHSPITZE
some grade III climbs
» 2,904 ft/885 m EG » 1.9 mi/3 km
» 4 h » difficult

TOUR 2 MÄDELEGABEL
Path to the Bockkarscharte → Heilbronner Weg. Steep step on the route to the summit
» 2,034 ft/620 m EG » 1.6 mi/2.5 km
» 3 h » difficult

TOUR 3 RAPPENSEEHÜTTE
Take the Heilbronner Weg over the Steinschartenkopf and Hohe Licht to the Rappenseehütte
» 1,640 ft/500 m EG » 3.2 mi/5.3 km
» 4 h » difficult

GERMANY | BAVARIA

On the Mountain River

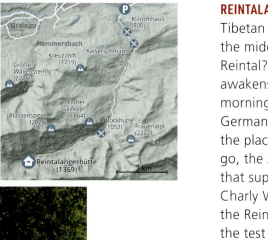

REINTALANGERHÜTTE Just a minute, Tibetan prayer flags are flying in the middle of the Upper Bavarian Reintal? Gentle guitar music awakens mountaineers early in the morning? And all this right near Germany's highest mountain and the place so many alpinists want to go, the Zugspitze? Some traditions that superhost and globetrotter Charly Wehrle has established in the Reintalangerhütte will stand the test of time and ensure a very special hut experience.

In 1912, the members of the Munich section of the Alpine Club built a shelter where the Partnach springs forth from the Zugspitzmassif. They could not have chosen a more picturesque location: It stands among dark firs in the middle of a forest clearing, the Wetterstein mountains rise majestically all around, and the headwaters of the Partnach gush past the front of the hut in a flat gravel bed. Generations of mountaineers have cast off their hiking boots here with a relieved sigh and cooled their tired feet in the crystal-clear mountain water. Whether your trail took you up the impressive Partnachklamm or down from the Zugspitze—the Reintalhütte is just the place for a long rest.

In the Middle Ages, shepherds drove their cattle into this idyllic section of the valley. However, its tranquility was threatened as enthusiasm for alpine sports increased. At the beginning of the 19th century, the conquerors

 Located directly on the rushing Partnach River, a stay at the Reintalangerhütte feels like you're on holiday.

GERMANY | BAVARIA | REINTALANGERHÜTTE

of the Zugspitze, Lieutenant Josef Naus and his mountain guide and companion, spent the night at this point on the river where there was already a small log cabin. One of their diary entries, however, tells less about the beauty of the landscape and more about the plague inside: Huge quantities of fleas deprived the climbers of sleep. The old building is no longer called the "flea hut." The fleas were quickly brought under control, and so numerous alpinists used the hut as an overnight camp on the way to the Zugspitze or other peaks in the Reintal. Until it was bursting at the seams. Today, the old hut of the new Reintalangerhütte is right next door. Together, the pair of huts defy the mountain weather, whose unpredictable moods have forced many climbers to step up their pace. So it's really nice when you can scurry under the protective roof of a hut that keeps the wind and rain at bay, and also warms your heart. The ascent is also suitable for families.

For many decades, the walls of the Reintalangerhütte have exuded a rustic coziness, nourished by happy and convivial hours spent in

IN BRIEF

VALLEY TOWN Garmisch-Partenkirchen

ALTITUDE 4,491 ft/1,369 m above sea level

OPEN end of May to mid-October

ACCOMMODATIONS 14 beds (shared rooms), 3 dbl rooms, 73-bed dormitory, 10 winter beds

FOOD hearty mountaineering food

GOOD TO KNOW Online reservation tool.

REINTALANGERHÜTTE | BAVARIA | GERMANY

You can make yourself comfortable in the Reintalangerhütte's pretty dormitories.

the lounge, which has hardly changed at all. The Reintalangerhütte has always been the beloved home of a dedicated mountain community. Anyone who has succumbed to its charms can't forget it. Many who have experienced the busy summer months here remain closely connected to this spot and return again and again, like the electrician, who has been repairing the hut's finicky technology for 30 years. The Reintalangerhütte is also a home away from home for the young hut hosts Andy Kiechle and Robert Schmon. They used to spend their holidays here; later, they worked as seasonal staff, and they have been an experienced hut hosting team since 2020. They know what it takes to keep this unique, historic flair alive on the banks of the Partnach.

TOURS

TOUR 1 **KREUZECKHAUS**
Reintalangerhütte → Bockhütte across the gentle Bernadeinsteig → Kreuzeckhaus at 5,420 feet (1,652 meters)
» 2,230 ft/680 m EG » 7.5 mi/12 km
» 5.5 h » easy

TOUR 2 **ZUGSPITZE**
Steep trail to the Zugspitzplatt, past the Knorrhütte and Schneefernerhaus over the SW ridge (with wire ropes) to the summit
» 5,249 ft/1,600 m EG » 4.7 mi/7.5 km
» 6–7 h » medium

TOUR 3 **HOCHWANNER**
Technically challenging tour to the Hochwanner - requires good conditioning and surefootedness (difficulty level I in places)
» 5,249 ft/1,600 m EG » 6.8 mi/11 km
» 7–8 h » difficult

In the middle of the barren Wetterstein Mountains, a golden cross marks the highest peak in Germany—the Zugspitze.

GERMANY | BAVARIA | REINTALANGERHÜTTE

"Melt, snow!"

Severe weather, wet snow avalanches, mudslides: The whims of nature shape life in the Reintal. Submitting to these powerful forces is usually the best idea—unless your name is Charly Wehrle. For 25 years, he was the host of the Reintalangerhütte, and as such had a problem when the snow blocked access roads. Out of necessity, he developed a system for defrosting avalanches. Initially, he melted small holes into the snow using garden hoses. Later, he replaced these with fire hoses and even cleared the way for his motorcycle.

When the sun shines, the Alpine snowbells' dark flower buds warm up more than their surroundings, so these delicate flowers can push themselves through the snow cover. This is a method that might interest Charly Wehrle.

REINTALANGERHÜTTE | BAVARIA | GERMANY

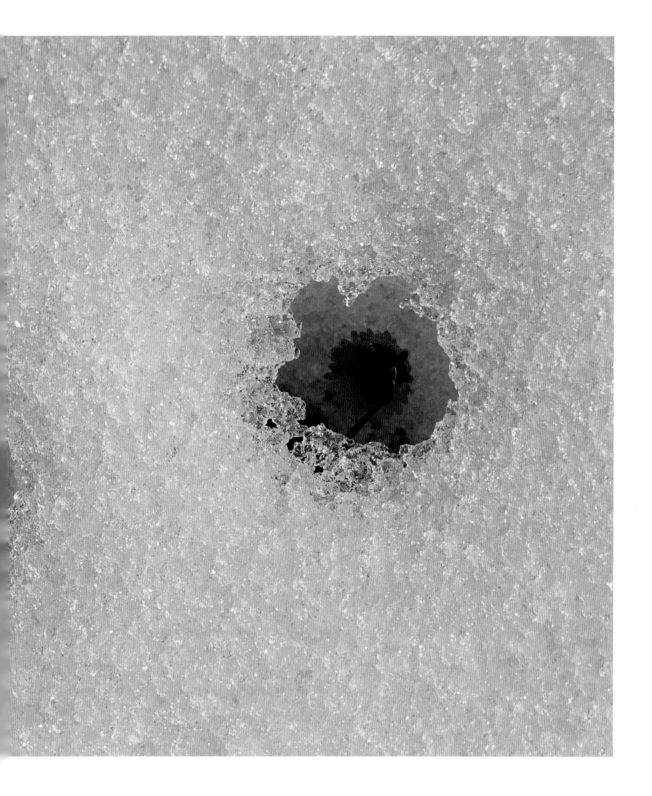

GERMANY | BAVARIA

18

The Highest One

The idyllic Weilheimer Hütte is located in the saddle between the Krottenkopf and Oberer Ri kopf.

WEILHEIMER HÜTTE The Weilheimer Hütte is the highest hut in the Bavarian foothills. It's located in the small, tranquil Ester Mountains between the Isar and Loisach Valleys near Garmisch-Partenkirchen. Here the Bavarian foothills are higher than everywhere else. On the Krottenkopf, the highest peak, you even cross the 6,561-foot (2,000-meter) mark.

We hardly know where to begin. The sun rises slowly from its night's rest above the peaks of the Karwendel Mountains and bathes everything in an orange light. At the same time, the crescent moon sinks over the Ammergebirge. It's a cold but exciting spectacle that takes place on the Krottenkopf.

Christian, the hut's host, had put us in the winter room so that we could get up early and hike across smooth stones to the summit to watch nature wake up from there. He understood what we wanted to do; after all, he himself is an enthusiastic nature photographer. Christian's calendar is a piece of the Weilheimer Hütte's beauty you can take home with you. Of course it's much nicer to experience it up close and personal.

However, we had our doubts as to whether the morning would be as impressive as we had imagined. On the ascent to the hut, the fog was so dense that we couldn't see 30 feet in front of us, and so we only saw the hut once we were standing directly in front of it. The slightly ghostly atmosphere led us to concluded that

117

GERMANY | BAVARIA | WEILHEIMER HÜTTE

the fog would not dissipate by morning. However, we were lucky: When we crawled out of our beds, the stars were still shining in the clear night sky.

It's not just the sunrises at the Weilheimer Hütte that are fabulous. It's also the food with which Christian pampers his guests. These are simple, tasty, lovingly prepared dishes. Only regional, truly local products make it onto the table with the "This is how mountains taste" seal of quality. And you can taste this! No matter if there is venison or pumpkin soup. As good as the food is, you should leave room for dessert; grandma's nut triangles, for example, are the perfect conclusion to a wonderful dinner.

By the end of his 20s, Christian had decided to be a hut host. Frequently, his workdays are as long as 16 hours. To survive this, you have to commit yourself heart and soul. With Christian, this is evident in the friendly and joyful way he welcomes his guests.

IN BRIEF

VALLEY TOWNS Garmisch-Partenkirchen, Oberau, Walgau, Farchant, Krün, Klais, Eschenlohe

ALTITUDE 6,414 ft/1,955 m above sea level

OPEN Pentecost to the 3rd Sunday in October

ACCOMMODATIONS 4 beds (shared rooms), 3 dbl rooms, 50-bed dormitory, 5 winter beds

FOOD ddelicious, simple, regional dishes

GOOD TO KNOW Reservations by telephone.

WEILHEIMER HÜTTE | BAVARIA | GERMANY

The idyllic village of Wallgau with the church St. Jakob in the Karwendel foothills.

From the summit of the Krottenkopf, you can see the Bischof and Wetterstein Mountains with the Zugspitze.

Definitely a reason to return to the Weilheimer Hütte again and again.

The trail to this cozy hut in the Ester Mountains is long, whichever way you come, and without an overnight stay in a hut, it would be quite tedious. But that's exactly why you should really absorb the hut experience. For then it doesn't matter that the beds are sometimes a little short and you're a bit cramped if you're taller than five foot ten. If you want to be even more solitary, climb up to the plateau to the NE of the hut and enjoy the deserted expanse there.

TOURS

TOUR 1 KROTTENKOPF
Short but steep ascent to the top of the Ester Mountains
» 295 ft/90 m EG » .3 mi/430 m
» 30 min » easy

TOUR 2 KUHFLUCHT WATERFALLS
Easy hike–it's mostly downhill. Beautiful forest adventure trail next to the waterfalls
» 98 ft/30 HM » 6.2 mi/10 km
» 4 h » easy

TOUR 3 WANKHAUS
Trail from hut to hut crosses the Hohe Fricken and most of the Ester Mountains.
» 2,395 ft/730 m EG » 6.2 mi/10 km
» 3.5 h » medium

HUT BOOK

Trend Transalp: Hiking from hut to hut: Beautiful and difficult

Crossing the Alps, hiking from hut to hut, has become one of the most popular activities for mountain lovers. The E5 from Oberstdorf to Merano is especially popular. From the Allgäu Alps in the Northern Alps, you pass through all kinds of mountain vegetation to the eternal ice in the Ötztal Alps. There, you visit the Ötzi site and then hike down to the southern Alps toward Merano. The final stage is a nice walk through this Italian city. In addition to this highly frequented route, there are other tours from hut to hut that are exciting and not quite so crowded. These include the Adlerweg from the Wilder Kaiser to the Arlberg, the Tiroler Höhenweg from the Zillertal to Merano, and the Via Alpina with its various trail variants.

For many hiking enthusiasts, crossing the Alps on the E5 begins in Oberstdorf in the Allgäu.

GERMANY | BAVARIA

The Kingly One

The fairy-tale king had a hunting lodge built on the romantic Soiernseen lakes in the Soiernkessel below the Soiernspitze.

SOIERNHAUS The Bavarian fairy-tale king Ludwig II knew exactly where it was beautiful in his Bavarian mountains. He had hunting lodges built in special places, and he enjoyed the beauty, tranquility, and seclusion of nature there. One of these former hunting lodges is the Soiernhaus of the Hochland section of the German Alpine Association.

It's Whit Monday, a beautiful sunny day. We're sitting on the terrace of the Soiernhaus at the edge of the magnificent Soiernkessel. Surprisingly, the hut is almost empty today. There are only two other guests here. Life is so relaxed that we can chat with the host on the terrace in peace. After a quiet night at the hut and an ample breakfast, we hike to the Fereinalm the next day and back into the valley.

The Schöttelkarspitze is also a summit that Ludwig liked to visit. That's why he built a pavilion up here and even had the summit taken down by a few feet. The path to the Soiernspitze is also called the bridle path—because of course the king didn't want to go to the summit on foot. But any search for the pavilion would be in vain. In addition to the beauty of nature and the lakes, the former hunting huts have been preserved. While the former horse stable is used by the mountain rescue service and is a self-catering hut in the Hochland section, the larger hut is operated as the Soiernhaus by the young hut hosts Klaus Heufelder and Susanne Härtl. Their guests praise these two for their fri-

GERMANY | BAVARIA | SOIERNHAUS

IN BRIEF

VALLEY TOWN Krün

ALTITUDE 5,301 ft/1,616 m above sea level

OPEN Pentecost to early October

ACCOMMODATIONS 60-bed dormitory, no multi-bed or double rooms

FOOD small menu, but large portions

GOOD TO KNOW The Soiernhaus has no winter room!

There is breathtaking scenery on the hike to the Soiernspitze: You can see the western Karwendelspitze, the Arnspitze, and the Wetterstein Mountains with the Zugspitze.

endly hospitality and delicious food. You should definitely leave some space in your stomach for the delicious nut triangles. Incidentally, the Lakaiensteig also dates back to the king's day. The servants shortened the ascent to the huts in order to prepare them for the king's arrival.

Of course, a lot has changed in the hut since then. An important milestone was the presentation of the DAV Environmental Seal in 2017; the Soiernhaus was only the tenth German Al¬pine Club hut to receive this award. Over the years, the section has put many hours of volunteer work into this project. The conversion of the combined heat and power plant from a diesel generator to environmentally friendly rapeseed oil was a crucial step toward making the hut more sustainable. Despite all the modernization, the Soiernhaus is still a cozy and authentic Bavarian mountain hut. There are modern toilets and cold running water in the washroom, but there are no showers, for example. Hikers sleep in dormitories, so you

SOIERNHAUS | BAVARIA | GERMANY

shouldn't be too sensitive to noise. However, it's extremely cozy and the experience of a hut stay there is particularly authentic.

The landscape is also wonderfully pristine, almost as it was in Ludwig's time. The mountain cirque with its two lakes is extraordinarily beautiful. The absolute highlight is the Soiernrundung, which begins at the Schöttelkarspitze and continues to the striking Soiernspitze. This is a panoramic hike, one on which you feel very close to the sky, which is unique in the Bavarian Alps. You always move along the exposed ridge edge and enjoy a magnificent view of the Karwendel and Wetterstein mountains.

TOURS

TOUR 1 HOCHLANDHÜTTE
You must be fit for this long scenic tour
» 3,478 ft/1,060 m EG » 6.84 mi/13 km
» 6 h » medium

TOUR 2 SCHÖTTELKARSPITZE
Wide path up to the summit; King Ludwig II was carried here in a litter
» 1,410 ft/430 m EG » 1.9 mi/3 km
» 1.5 h » medium

TOUR 3 GUMPEN & KRAPFENKAR
Panoramic ridge hike to little-visited peaks. Path is not marked and is not on maps; for experienced hikers only
» 2,296 ft/700 m EG » 3.7 mi/6 km
» 3 h » difficult

A popular hike to the Soiernhaus leads from the parking lot in Krün across the Fischbachalm, which is at an altitude of 4,593 feet.

GERMANY | BAVARIA | SOIERNHAUS

Rheingold on the lakes

King Ludwig II wasn't just a lover of the Bavarian mountains, he knew their special places. He also loved operas by Richard Wagner and got some strange ideas from them, as illustrated by his fairytale castles, among other things.

One story says that he once traveled across the lakes of the Soiernhaus in a dragon boat on a moonlit night, having musicians by the lakeside play pieces from *Das Rheingold*. Mountain fires lit by his servants on the surrounding peaks ensured majestic scenery.

Servants had to carry the boat all the way from the valley for this purpose. However, it's unclear whether this story is true. Divers have not found any remains of a dragon boat in the lakes. But who knows what kind crazy ideas the king actually had.

Because King Ludwig II was a huge Richard Wagner fan, he had himself painted as Lohengrin—the main character of the Wagner opera by the same name.

126

SOIERNHAUS | BAVARIA | GERMANY 🇩🇪

GERMANY | BAVARIA

20

The Eagle's Nest

TEGERNSEER HÜTTE It's already a very impressive location for an Alpine Club hut. The small Tegernseer Hütte sits like an eagle's nest between the two imposing rock peaks Roßstein and Buchstein in the Bavarian upland between Lenggries and the Tegernsee. The view from the sunny hut terrace—to the south to the mighty Guffert—and on clear days even to the ice giants of the Central Alps—is accordingly magnificent.

When you step out of the forest at the Sonnbergalm, you will immediately see the two rocky peaks of the Roßstein and Buchstein, which tower majestically over hikers. Right in the middle of all this is the unique location of the small Tegernseer Hütte, which is perched right on the precipice like an eagle's nest.

But how can you climb the steep cliffs to get there? Not infrequently, hikers feel queasy at that moment. But nothing changes if you stand by the rock face below the Roßstein. Hikers use the wire ropes for the ascent, and here it's essential that you not be afraid of heights. Only when you reach the hut can you relax. Then you saunter the last few feet to the Tegernseer Hütte, where Michl, the hospitable hut host, will serve you a well-deserved snack and a cool drink. This quickly banishes your misgivings and fears.

When this hut was built at the beginning of the 20th century, there was no cable car for transporting the building materials to the

Early risers are rewarded on the Roßstein when the morning sun slowly rises behind the sleepy mountain world and turns everything a soft red.

GERMANY | BAVARIA | TEGERNSEER HÜTTE

IN BRIEF

VALLEY TOWN Bayerwald bei Kreuth

ALTITUDE 5,413 ft/1,650 m above sea level

OPEN early May to early November

ACCOMMODATIONS 2 dormitories with 23 beds, no double rooms

FOOD simple menu with mountaineering food; additional dish for overnight guests

GOOD TO KNOW Often very crowded on the weekend.

The goal is already in sight: The Tegernseer Hütte appears between the Buchstein and Roßstein.

mountain. Instead, everything had to be carried by hand. The fact that a wooden door weighing 115 kg was hauled up the mountain by a 18-year-old apprentice all by himself still amazes hut guests. Today there is a cozy shelter up here, which has lost none of its original character despite several renovations. Supply and disposal is, of course, important in such a location. Water is an especially scarce commodity between the two limestone peaks. This means that the hut is supplied exclusively by rainwater, which is sterilized in an environmentally friendly manner with a UV system. To avoid wasting too much water, there are only dry toilets up here. The hut is heated with wood from local forests, and a thermal solar system heats water for the kitchen.

The breathtaking view from the hut invites you to dream, to dream of the great mountains on the other side of the German border. The ice giants of the Central Alps form a gorgeous line from here. The only catch: Frequently, you will have to share the panorama and hut's location with many like-minded people.

TEGERNSEER HÜTTE | BAVARIA | GERMANY

The coveted viewpoints on the terrace are also very popular. Therefore, you'll be better off if you visit the Tegernseer Hütte during the week, when there is more peace and quiet than on weekends and holidays.

If you want to fully enjoy the hut experience, stay overnight up here. Especially on a balmy summer evening, the west terrace invites you to enjoy a wonderful sunset before you indulge in the delicious dinner, which can be vegetarian if you wish.

In the hut itself you will find a relaxed atmosphere, and you will feel like the hut hosts, Michl and Sylvia, are your family. This makes up for the scant space in the dormitory, where things can get quite cuddly.

TOURS

TOUR 1 GUFFERTHÜTTE
Trail across the scenic Blaubergkamm. Long tour requires good conditioning; start on time
» 4,360 ft/1,329 m EG » 12.1 mi/19.5 km » 7 h » medium

TOUR 2 LENGGRIESER HÜTTE
Short crossing has it all: mountain ridges, forests, and rocky passages. Take a side trip to the Seekarkarkreuz summit
» 614 ft/187 m EG » 3.5 mi/5.7 km » 2.5 h » medium

TOUR 3 BUCHSTEIN
Smooth gully requires climbing skills (difficulty level I–II) → summit.
» 164 ft/50 m EG » 0.1 mi/100 m » 1 h » difficult

The hut's namesake is the Tegernsee, which has been named "Bavaria's favorite lake" for years.

GERMANY | BAVARIA | TEGERNSEER HÜTTE

Via Wheat Beer

Suddenly, one hand, then two hands, and finally a face appear at the edge of the hut's terrace. We look at the edge in shock. A climber comes up and greets us with a friendly "Servus."

The surprise was probably written on our faces. But this isn't so rare. After all, the last stage of the Via Wheat Beer climbing route ends on the terrace of the Tegernseer Hütte.

We relax when the climber doesn't succumb to the temptation to challenge us for our wheat beer but instead secures his companion and thus ends his climbing tour properly. Only then does he call the host to order a cool drink to refresh himself and his friend.

→ Regular climbing improves endurance, stability, flexibility, agility, spatial perception, hand-eye coordination, and, of course, balance. Those who approach the terrace via the climbing route must be experienced.

TEGERNSEER HÜTTE | BAVARIA | GERMANY

GERMANY | BAVARIA

The Summit Hut

REICHENHALLER HAUS The Reichenhaller Haus is located just a few feet below the summit of the Hochstaufen in the Chiemgau Mountains. The hut is especially popular with day visitors, because the Hochstaufen is easily accessible from several sides. You can enjoy a magical experience by staying up here in simplicity.

We came via the Steinerner Jäger trail to reach the summit of Hochstaufen for the first time from Bad Reichenhall. Fog wafts around us and limits the view. However, the path is well-marked and therefore easy to find. Nevertheless, we are a bit concerned about our summit outlook. As the fog clears, we see the Reichenhaller Haus in front of us, just a stone's throw away from the summit of the Hochstaufen. So before we stop at the hut, we make a quick stop at the summit cross. After we take a good look around the summit—now beautiful without fog—then it's time to proceed to the hut.

The hut hosts Christine and Andreas spoil us with simple but delicious dishes. Andreas carries fresh ingredients to the hut several times a week in his frame backpack. There is no material cableway. In the past, the hut was supplied with mules by the Bundeswehr; today there are supply flights by helicopter from time to time, especially for materials that go beyond everyday needs.

Overall, the Reichenhaller Haus is a rather simple mountain hut. There are no showers, only sinks. The outdoor toilet offers a rainwater barel

Just a few feet below the Hochstaufen summit stands the Reichenhaller Haus; it's blessed with a great view of the Salzachtal.

GERMANY | BAVARIA | REICHENHALLER HAUS

for washing hands. Water is a scarce commodity up here. A rainwater collection system ensures the water supply, but it is very exposed to the weather. We like the simplicity here; after all, there are already too many "mountain hotels" in the Alps.

And the view from the hut makes up for everything anyway. Salzburg, Bad Reichenhall, and the Chiemsee are at your feet, and you can't get enough of looking down and admiring the landscape. The beginning and the end of the day are spectacles here that you simply shouldn't miss. In the morning, the sun climbs over the Salzkammergut, and in the evening it seems to sink directly into the Chiemsee. The terrace of the Reichenhaller Haus is, of course, all guests' favorite place. In addition to these impressive daily moments, there is another special event every year near the Reichenhaller Haus. A few steps away from the hut is the Staufenkapelle, built at the end of the 1920s.

As a rule, the famous Staufenmesse is held here on the first Sunday after the summer solstice—if weather conditions permit. And on the evening before, the Staufenfreunde provide some magical moments when they light small fires at the summit, at the Reichenhaller Haus, and at the chapel.

The summit of the Hochstaufen (above) is 5,813 feet high and can be called Bad Reichenhall's "local mountain" (below).

IN BRIEF

VALLEY TOWN Bad Reichenhall or Piding

ALTITUDE 5,741 ft/1,750 m above sea level

OPEN mid-May to mid-October

ACCOMMODATIONS 6 beds in multi-bed rooms and 12-bed dormitory

FOOD Food is supplied by helicopter or by the host personally, which is why the menu is relatively small but very tasty

GOOD TO KNOW Hut sleeping bag is mandatory, hut quiet hours from 10 p.m. to 6 a.m., payment only in cash.

REICHENHALLER HAUS | BAVARIA | GERMANY

On the day of the mass, numerous visitors come to celebrate in the church. After this, you can sit on the terrace for a long time and enjoy the view and hospitality with traditional live music from local musical groups.

There are many ways to get to the Reichenhaller Haus. The Steinerner Jäger trail is one of two normal routes from the south. It's a bit more challenging than the trail across the Barthlmahd, but it's still good for experienced hikers despite the rocky passages.

TOURS

TOUR 1 ZWIESELALM
The closest hut is the Zwieselalm, with one of the most beautiful views of Bad Reichenhall. It can be reached via a demanding tour over the Zwiesel (see below) or there is an easier trail across the Barthlmahd
» 492 ft/150 m EG » 2.7 mi/43 km
» 2 h » medium

TOUR 2 MITTELSTAUFEN & ZWIESEL
This panoramic ridge hike begins at the Hochstaufen and leads on several wire ropes across the Mittelstaufen and Zennokopf to Zwiesel
» 1,082 ft/330 m EG » 2.5 mi/4 km
» 2 h » difficult

The Staufenkapelle right next to the Reichenhaller Haus invites you to take a short break.

GERMANY | BAVARIA | REICHENHALLER HAUS

A sad chapter

The Reichenhaller Haus was the scene of a sad chapter in the history of the German Alpine Club. In September 1993, two Croatian youths fled from a juvenile prison to the Hochstaufen. On their way there, they committed several robberies. After ordering a drink in the hut, they shot one of the hosts in cold blood. A little later, they killed the other host too. Their "take" was 1,500 DM ($800 USD) and a little food. It's hard to believe that someone would take human lives for this. The two robbers were arrested in Zagreb a short time later. However, this didn't bring the hosts back. A memorial plaque at the Reichenhaller Haus commemorates their murder.

→

Twilight is a good time to remember the two deceased hosts of the Reichenhaller Haus.

REICHENHALLER HAUS | BAVARIA | GERMANY

🇦🇹 AUSTRIA

Kaiserschmarrn and glaciers, Tyrolian bacon and mountain lakes: Austria's huts entice hikers with their outstanding cuisine and unique landscape. And the huts could not be more varied. There are very modern huts equipped with WiFi and boulder rooms, and there are authentic, rustic wood-paneled huts, where it doesn't bother anyone that there's only cold water and you have to share a dormitory with many like-minded people.

We head to the Ötztal and the king of the Austrian mountains—the Großglockner—and meet marmots at the Floitengrund and enjoy spectacular sunsets in the Verwall Mountains. There are curiosities such as the magnificent chandelier in the so-called "Alpine Castle," but in many places the attraction is primarily the hospitality of the hut hosts and staff.

Nestled in the Zillertal Alps, the man-made Schlegeis Reservoir is at an altitude of almost 5,905 feet above sea level.

AUSTRIA | VORARLBERG

The Unknown One

The Saarbrücker Hütte—the highest refuge in the Silvetta—makes a friendly impression from afar with its facade made of wooden shingles and its blue-and-white painted shutters.

SAARBRÜCKER HÜTTE While the Silvretta is a popular area for hikers and mountaineers, the Saarbrücker Hütte, located in this region, is less well-known. It has neither a popular summit destination, nor is it developed like a hotel. But that's exactly what makes it interesting. How wonderful it is to enjoy the lonely mountain world in a rarely crowded and yet extremely cozy hut.

The gravel road up is tedious, especially if you have decided to bring bicycles. There are no shade trees here. However, when you finally make your way home after a great stay at the Saarbrücker Hütte, you will know that every drop of sweat was worth it. Without much effort, you speed downhill to the Silvretta High Alpine Road and spare yourself the tiring descent. Life is sublime when the wind whistles around your ears and the mountain panorama changes a bit with every meter.

But you shouldn't think about going home right away. Once at the top, guests are first greeted by a magnificent view of the impressive pair of peaks, the Großlitzner and Großseehorn; their crossing is one of the most beautiful two-peak tours in the Silvretta Mountains. Admittedly, the summit of the Großlitzner doesn't look very welcoming. Things look a bit better the next day. We only put on our climbing shoes for a short stretch below the summit. On the other hand, abseiling makes us very happy. And then we re-

AUSTRIA | VORARLBERG | SAARBRÜCKER HÜTTE

IN BRIEF

VALLEY TOWN Partenen

ALTITUDE 8,327 ft/2,538 m above sea level

OPEN mid-June to end of September

ACCOMMODATIONS 23 beds in multi-bed rooms, 7 double rooms, 51-bed dormitory, 12-bed winter room

FOOD regional dishes, especially dumplings, some seasonal

GOOD TO KNOW The host can only be reached by telephone; cash only; hot showers on request

Fighting Alpine marmots can injure each other quite badly with their sharp teeth.

For Stefan Schöpf, his dream came true when he took over the hut. Initially, he chose to work as a mason and carpenter, but he explored the mountain world whenever time allowed. He was also able to pursue his passion for summits as a mountain rescuer. When there was a search for a host for the Saarbrücker Hütte in 2017, Stefan seized the opportunity and he doesn't regret this decision one bit. During the summer months, his entire family, including the children, lives in the hut. His brother-in-law serves as the chef, preparing Kaiserschmarrn, dumplings, and such. By the way, everything is cooked fresh, without a deep fryer and according to traditional recipes. And you can taste that!

If you want to hike the stage to the Tübinger Hütte the next morning, you can sleep in, for the trail is not long. You could have hiked through and skipped the Saarbrücker Hütte altogether, but that would have been a pity, because then you would have missed the hut hospitality of the Unknown One.

turn to the Saarbrücker Hütte. Here, refreshment awaits exhausted hikers. The family and staff of Stefan Schöpf, the hut host, take great care of their guests. Their cordial manner and readiness to help are real. The kitchen is known for its spinach dumplings and Kaspressknödel (pressed cheese dumpling) soup. Depending on the season, there may also be delicious Rohnenknödel—beetroot dumplings—or chanterelle dumplings.

The hut's coziness has not changed in recent years, in contrast to the glacier, which is shrinking. Everyone will spend the evening together in the lounge, talking about great routes and exciting experiences in the mountains and looking forward to the next day. If you want to refresh yourself before going to bed, there's even a shower in the hut—not a matter of course in the Alps. However, it is cold; there's only warm water if you order ahead.

SAARBRÜCKER HÜTTE | VORARLBERG | AUSTRIA

From May to July, the evergreen shrub of the hairy alpenrose features beautiful flowers.

TOURS

TOUR 1 KLEINES SEEHORN
Ski tour: Saarbrücker Hütte -> Schweizer Lücke -> Kleines Seehorn, best in April
» 1,640 ft/500 m EG   » 2.5 mi/4 km
» 2.5 h   » medium

TOUR 2 TÜBINGER HÜTTE
Tour across the Kromertal and Hochmadererjoch requires endurance. Stay over in the Tübinger Hütte
» 2,625 ft/800 m EG   » 8.1 mi/13 km
» 6.5 h   » medium

TOUR 3 KLEINLITZNER
The Kleinlitzner via ferrata features a fabulous view of the Silvretta. Topographical maps on sale in the hut
» 590 ft/180 m EG   » 0.6 mi/1 km
» 2 h   » medium

The Kleinlitzner is a peak that precedes the glacial ten-thousand footers in the Silvretta and offers a great view.

— AUSTRIA | VORARLBERG | SAARBRÜCKER HÜTTE

Ski races at the Saarbrücker Hütte

In the 1950s, about 40 skiers ran a real ski race at the Saarbrücker Hütte each year in April. The starting point was the Saarbrücker Hütte, which is at an altitude of 8,327 feet. In April, the snow is often soft early in the day, which makes the descent difficult. In addition, there's a danger of avalanches. The old equipment was also no match for today's high-tech skis: Wooden skis had virtually no edges, and bindings were just straps that remained firmly attached to the hiking boot even when falling. This made motivation all the greater! Through the Komertal, past Lake Vermuntsee to Partenen, the racers sped down the almost 4,925 feet of elevation gain (or loss, in this case).

When ski jumping was in its infancy, athletes had to make do with wooden skis.

SAARBRÜCKER HÜTTE | VORARLBERG | AUSTRIA

AUSTRIA | VORARLBERG

23

The Romantic One

KALTENBERGHÜTTE An ambiance as if from a holiday catalog: While the sun sinks behind the Swiss mountains, overnight guests will wake up with a beautiful view of the Klostertal and the peaks of the Lechquellen Mountains. The Kaltenberghütte on the Bludenzer Alp offers just the right setting to enjoy such romantic moments in style.

The Reutlingen Alpine Club section has renovated a lot in recent years. In addition to romantic hut rooms, there are now also modern dormitories in the new building next door and a terrace with lounge chairs like the ones on a sun deck. The power supply was also modernized, so that the hut was awarded the Alpine Association's environmental seal. Water comes from a spring, a solar system generates electricity, and a new material cableway was built for transport; it's powered by an environmentally friendly rapeseed oil unit. There is also a seminar room up here—less romantic, perhaps, but practical.

In the past, skiers used the Kaltenberghütte as a base, but since the hut had to be rebuilt after a fire, it has also been very popular in summer. Families with children especially like to come here. Due to the possibilities for younger guests, the German Alpine Association has officially named it a "child-friendly hut." Is it the horses that graze nearby and come in for caresses, the climbing rocks, or the little lakes that invite you to swim? Life here will certainly never be boring. And furthermore: Which hut has

Situated high above the Klostertal, the Kaltenberghütte offers beautiful views from its airy, open balcony-like location.

149

AUSTRIA | VORARLBERG | KALTENBERGHÜTTE

the highest swimming lake in this region? At more than 6,560 feet, water lovers can take the plunge and end their long days of hiking with natural mountain cooling. Anyone who enjoys the last rays of sunshine on the expansive panoramic terrace and—for romance's sake, arm-in-arm with a partner—watches the sunset light up the surrounding mountains, will certainly never want to leave here again.

Unless someone calls them for dinner. In the evening, hut host Markus Kegele and his team spoil their guests with a three-course menu and put regional home cooking on the table. The ingredients all come from the surrounding region and preferably from organic farms. All the hut's guests come together in the large dining room and enjoy their time on the mountain—regardless of whether they have come here as seminar participants or as mountain athletes or are traveling with children. The atmosphere in the hut is so relaxed and

IN BRIEF

VALLEY TOWN Stuben am Arlberg, Langen, St. Christoph

ALTITUDE 6,854 ft/2,089 m above sea level

OPEN end of June to end of September

ACCOMMODATIONS romantic rooms and idyllic multi-bed rooms, 22-bed dormitory, 14-bed winter room

FOOD regional specialties with local ingredients, vegetarian options

GOOD TO KNOW don't forget your swimsuit

KALTENBERGHÜTTE | VORARLBERG | AUSTRIA

Horses run free in front of the Kaltenbergerhütte—to the great delight of the little hut guests. (top)

Since the flowers of these alpine cowbells are bright sulfur yellow, they are also called sulfur anemones. (below)

Although the name Berggeistweg ("mountain spirit trail") might suggest ghosts, there are none; just fresh mountain air and awesome views.

open that frequently conversations develop between people who rarely meet in the real world. A hut stay like this brings people together. Anyone who has brought their favorite people along will also appreciate the romantic atmosphere of the hut and its surroundings. There's something for everyone.

The morning is as tasty as the evening was social. The first highlight of the day is the mountain breakfast with crispy hut bread, buttery plaited braid, homemade jam, local cheese, homemade muesli, and a glass of Prosecco. After breakfast, some people seek alpine adventure near the hut. And the others? They grab their suits and go for a swim.

TOURS

TOUR 1 **KONSTANZER HÜTTE**
Hike the Berggeistweg to the mountain station of the Albona Bahn, the Maroijoch and Maroital, and the Schönverwalltal
» 1,378 ft/420 m EG   » 9 mi/14.5 km
» 6 h   » medium

TOUR 2 **KRACHELSPITZE**
Walk below the Alpenkopf to the Krachel before the terrain gets steeper in the notch. Narrow trail to the beautiful summit cross
» 1,739 ft/530 m EG   » 2.5 mi/4 km
» 2 h   » medium

TOUR 3 **VERWALL ROUND**
Challenging 6-day tour on marked mountain trails takes you to 5 huts. You may hike as much as 9 hours a day
» 18,438 ft/5,620 m EG   » 41.6 mi/67 km
» 33 h   » difficult

AUSTRIA | VORARLBERG | KALTENBERGHÜTTE

"The sunsets at the Kaltenberghütte are legendary and offer a first-class spectacle in the fall. Most often, sunset happens shortly after dinner, as a kind of "dessert" after meatloaf, stuffed pasta, cheese spätzli, and sweet yeast rolls. The best place is the hut's popular terrace. This natural wonder is particularly impressive when the Klostertal lies under dense cloud cover and the evening sky turns yellow and then fire engine red. Then you don't want to be anywhere else but up here."

Quote by Helmut Kober, honorary chairman of the DAV section Reutlingen

KALTENBERGHÜTTE | VORARLBERG | AUSTRIA

AUSTRIA | TYROL

24

Above the Sea of Glaciers

BRANDENBURGER HAUS The Brandenburger Haus is the highest hut in the Ötztal Alps at an altitude of more than 10,498 feet; it's on a rock outcropping at the foot of the Dahmannspitze. The builders could not have chosen a more impressive location. Two mighty glaciers, the Gepatschferner and the Kesselwandferner, surround the rocks on which the hut is built and provide a great ambiance.

Slowly the sun sinks behind the mountain peaks of the Ötztal Alps. It bathes the glacier landscape in its orange light and fills the viewer's heart with a pleasant warmth—despite the deep snow and icy air. It's a wonderful place for this spectacle, probably one of the most beautiful in the Eastern Alps. You almost think you're in another world. And that's no wonder, for the nearest town is 6.2 miles away as the crow flies. And the hut stands like an island in a sea of ice in the middle of an inhospitable, yet fascinating glacier landscape.

For more than 100 years, the Brandenburger Haus has presided over the rocky promontory of the Dahmannspitze, just a few feet below the summit. It was named after the architect Dahmann—because planning and building a hut here is a great achievement, one that deserves special recognition.

For a hut at this altitude, the Brandenburger Haus is extremely comfortable: The wood-paneled dining room and tiled stove help visitors

Mountaineers whose destination is the Brandenburger Haus should be sure they are equipped with ropes, picks, and climbing irons.

AUSTRIA | TYROL | BRANDENBURGER HAUS

IN BRIEF

VALLEY TOWNS Vent in Ötztal and Feichten in Kaunertal

ALTITUDE 10,751 ft/2,089 m above sea level

OPEN end of June to mid-September

ACCOMMODATIONS 31 beds in multi-bed rooms, 46-bed dormitory, 6 emergency berths, no double rooms

FOOD simple, down-to-earth Austrian dishes

GOOD TO KNOW Split the ascent and spend a night in the Hochjoch-Hospiz

feel right at home. Just after sunset, when it gets cooler outside, the stove is a welcome source of heat. There's no shower up here, but the hut's fantastic location makes up for this—no hotel in the valley can compete with it.

It's impressive that the Brandenburger Haus received the environmental seal of approval from the German Alpine Club early on, in 2008. Extensive technology generates solar power and gathers and stores drinking water. The hut is heated exclusively with wood, a renewable raw material. This makes up at least a little for the unfortunately necessary supply by helicopter.

Such details don't let even less experienced guests forget that maintaining a mountain hut is not an easy task. The relatively frequent change of hut hosts emphasizes this. But the comparatively short time in which the hut is hosted annually does not lack amenities. After all, if you have fought your way around the many twists and turns of the Delorette Trail, then you also have—as a precaution—always roped up, because the crevasses are becoming more and more treacherous due to the glacier's

BRANDENBURGER HAUS | TYROL | AUSTRIA

decline. Once you have successfully conquered the Kesselwandferner, you will be happy about the little things in (hut) life. In the "glacier castle," as people in the region affectionately call the hut, the hut host's hospitality and hearty home cooking await you. In the morning, hikers don't have to make their way on an empty stomach, of course; an ample breakfast is provided. The hut is also available as a shelter for ski tourers when it is not hosted; it's not locked up.

TOURS

TOUR 1 HINTEREISSPITZEN
Easy but long high-altitude ski tour. Crosses the 3 Hintereisspitzen; magnificent glacier panoramas
» 984 ft/300 m EG   » 3.9 mi/6.3 km
» 6 h   » medium

TOUR 2 RAUHEKOPFHÜTTE
Flat route across the Gepatschferner; do not underestimate its crevasses
» 98 ft/30 HM   » 4.2 mi/6.8 km
» 2 h   » easy

TOUR 3 KESSELWANDSPITZE
Only for experienced high mountaineers; challenging tour across the Kesselwandgletscher to the Kesselwandspitze
» 885 ft/270 m EG   » 1.6 mi/2.6 km
» 3 h   » difficult

A worthwhile day tour from the Brandenburger Haus crosses the 3 Hintereisspitzen.

157

AUSTRIA | TYROL | BRANDENBURGER HAUS

Goats on the hut´s terrace

A few years ago, a climber was amazed to see a goat on the terrace of the Brandenburger Haus after he had been basking in the sun on the Dahmannspitze. Before he knew it, there were four goats. However, they were not helping to supply the hosts, but simply followed a group of hikers across the glacier. All attempts to take them back toward the Hochjoch-Hospiz were in vain.

Only in the evening did a hiker and his daughter manage to lead the goats across the glacier and along the Delorette Trail to the Hochjoch-Hospiz. Two of these stubborn animals were on a leash, the other two followed his daughter.

Hardly any other animal is as famous for its proverbial stubbornness as the goat.

BRANDENBURGER HAUS | TYROL | AUSTRIA

159

AUSTRIA | TYROL

25

Home of the Ibex

The Rüsselsheimer Hütte has a priceless view of the Kaunergrat across the way.

RÜSSELSHEIMER HÜTTE High above the narrow Pitztal, it stands on the Geigenkamm—the Rüsselsheimer Hütte, which had an entirely different name until a few years ago. In addition to a great summit, one of the hut's attractions are its unusual guests: A colony of ibex come to visit often, delighting the humans.

You may still find the hut's former name on old maps: Chemnitzer Hütte. However, after the Chemnitz section dissolved itself in 1973, the hut was transferred to the Rüsselsheim section. As part of its 75th anniversary celebration, it was finally renamed accordingly.

Since then, a lot has changed here. A great deal of work has been done to create a forward-looking, environmentally compatible power supply. The hut has a solar system, battery system, small hydropower plant, inverter system, combined heat and power plant with rapeseed oil, and combination stoves with wood pellets for hot water supply, electricity, and heating. The drinking water comes from a spring, and the wastewater is filtered in a special facility. Due to these exemplary environmental protection measures, the hut was awarded the environmental seal of approval in 2005.

Fortunately, other things have not changed. For example, the food continues to be excellent. At the Rüsselsheimer Hütte, you can enjoy delicious dumplings made from spinach, cheese, and bacon, as well as ibex carpaccio and gou-

AUSTRIA | TYROL | RÜSSELSHEIMER HÜTTE

lash. You can quench your thirst with a spicy, sweet beverage creation called "Meister Sepp." The Rüsselsheimer Hütte is part of the "This is how the mountains taste" campaign launched by the German Alpine Association in 1999. This seal of approval promotes the cooperation of hut hosts and regional food producers, especially mountain farmers. The guests of the Rüsselsheimer Hütte can see for themselves that good quality and local origin are not just buzzwords in the context of such a campaign; you really can taste the difference.

Both the flora and fauna around the hut are impressive—silver thistles, willow herb, and larkspur grow in the beautiful mountain meadows, for example—and lots of ibex live nearby. And they like to come close to the hut—especially at dusk, when it's quiet and they can be observed, as if they know that with their imposing horns and climbing talent, they are the secret stars of the Rüsselsheimer Hütte.

IN BRIEF

VALLEY TOWN Plangeross

ALTITUDE 7,621 ft/2,323 m above sea level

OPEN mid-June to end of September

ACCOMMODATIONS 1 double room, 10 beds in multi-bed rooms, 35-bed dormitory, 12-bed winter room

FOOD excellent Tyrolean cuisine; delicious dumplings, ibex carpaccio, and goulash

GOOD TO KNOW Playground with swing and a slackline; other play equipment in front of the hut

RÜSSELSHEIMER HÜTTE | TYROL | AUSTRIA

The alpine ibex is a frequent and welcome guest at the Rüsselsheimer Hütte. (top)

The most popular route to the Hohe Geige leads across the Westgrat. (below)

The reward for ascending to the highest peak of the Geigenkamm—the Hohe Geige—is the incredible view.

Anyone who is now surprised that hut host Florian Kirschner puts ibex goulash and carpaccio on the menu can be reassured: "If we do not hunt the ibex, there will be too many of them and they will displace the chamois." The ibex must be hunted either way.

Climbing enthusiasts will get their money's worth at the Rüsselsheimer Hütte, because there are numerous bouldering rocks, some beautiful climbing gardens, and a great practice via ferrata nearby. The Mainzer Höhenweg is also worthwhile. It runs from the Rüsselsheimer Hütte along a very demanding route to the Rheinland-Pfalz-Biwak and on to the Braunschweiger Hütte in the distant Pitztal.

TOURS

TOUR 1 WEISSMAURACHSEE
Hike the the Mainzer Höhenweg to the glacial lake below the Weißmaurachjoch
» 656 ft/200 m EG   » 1.2 mi/2 km
» 2 h   » easy

TOUR 2 KLEINBÄRENZINNE
Short practice via ferrata in a high alpine landscape; good for beginners
» 984 ft/300 m EG   » 1.5 mi/2.5 km
» 1.5 h   » medium

TOUR 3 HOHE GEIGE
Marked path to Gahwinden; Westgrat begins with a difficulty level II climb. Steel cables help hikers over the most difficult areas. Go back down the Westgrat; many other trails are not safe
» 3,510 ft/1,070 m EG   » 5.0 mi/8 km
» 7 h   » difficult

HUT BOOK

Taste of the mountains

High-altitude delicacies

The German Alpine Association's "This is how the mountains taste" campaign has been a great success. The initiative now extends across three countries and 40 mountain ranges, from the Schlernbödelehütte in the Dolomites to the Hochrieshütte in the Chiemgau Alps.

Classic alpine specialties that are often found in outstanding huts are, for example, Speck or Kaspressknödelsuppe (bacon or pressed cheese dumpling soup), Kässspatzn (cheese späzli, a special kind of egg noodles with cheese), Kaiserschmarrn (sweet shredded pancakes with fruit) or Älplermagronen (Swiss mac and cheese with potatoes) in Switzerland. But special dishes are also served in some huts. For example, there are Moosbeernocken (cranberry dumplings) at the Hallerangerhaus, Brennnesselknödel (nettle dumplings) at the Weilheimer Hütte, and vegan Bolognese at the Gamshütte. Some exotic dishes are also served. A few years ago, guests were amazed when they were served Nepalese food at the Sudetendeutsche Hütte. The hut host Ang Kami Lama and his kitchen staff have since moved to the Stuttgarter Hütte in the Lechtal Alps.

You're likely to start drooling at the sight of these Austrian spinach dumplings garnished with cheese.

165

AUSTRIA | TYROL

26

Hamburg's Highest

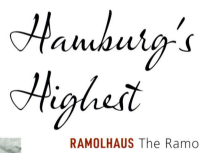

RAMOLHAUS The Ramolhaus is at an altitude of more than 9,842 feet above Obergurgl in the remotest part of the Ötztal. It's the tallest building in the otherwise flat Elbe metropolis since it belongs to the German Alpine Association's Hamburg section. Its location on a ledge directly above the valley is quite impressive. An overnight stay in this hut is one of the absolute highlights in the Ötztal.

← The mountain world slowly awakens from its sleep in the light of the warm morning sun. You can see the Ramolhaus and the awesome Gurgler Ferner.

It's a very long climb from Obergurgl. We drag ourselves uphill in the hot August sun. We leave ourselves a lot of time, but we still clearly notice the altitude. We've been training diligently for this trip lately, but we're still very happy when we finally reach the hut's terrace and move into our camp. The climb took us a little over four hours. But with that, two of us have not had not enough. They go on to climb the Hintere Spiegelkogel, the hut's local mountain. It towers almost 1,312 feet over them and is accessible without glaciers. The Ramolhaus has stood amidst this impressive scenery at a height of just over 9,842 feet since 1881. The architect and builder was Martin Scheiber, who built the first hut in the Ötztal Alps. Even today, Scheiber's descendants take care of the hut. Now it belongs to the Alpine Association, but it is hosted by Lukas Scheiber, Martin's great-grandson. However, since the family also owns a large hotel in the valley, the hut is managed by its own team. Despite many modernizations, the

AUSTRIA | TYROL | RAMOLHAUS

interior of the Ramolhaus offers a pleasant blend of comfort and coziness. You can enjoy the evening in the snug dining rooms and spend the night in comfortable shared rooms. Here everything is made of wood; the floor, walls, ceiling, and bunk beds. This makes the rooms extremely cozy and inviting. Equipped with soft pillows and warm blankets, the beds at the Ramolhaus promise a restful night's sleep. In the morning, hopefully the sun will wake you up, because in fine weather, breakfast—consisting of bread, a spread of some kind, and coffee or juice—is served on the terrace, and you can enjoy the magnificent view while you're eating.

Even during the day, you'll be well cared for up here. The large portions of schnitzel and dumplings in particular attract many regular guests. Ingredients come from the hut host's stock and organic farmers nearby, so they are very local. However, even though the schnitzel tastes so good, you should definitely save some room for the delicious desserts. It will be difficult to choose between the apple strudel and sweet

IN BRIEF

VALLEY TOWN Obergurgl in the Ötztal

ALTITUDE 9,862 ft/3,006 m above sea level

OPEN end of June to mid-September

ACCOMMODATIONS 18 beds in multi-bed rooms, 34-bed dormitory, winter room

FOOD Good Tyrolean cooking, 3-course dinner

GOOD TO KNOW Backpack transport with material cableway on request

RAMOLHAUS | TYROL | AUSTRIA

The dormitories of the Ramolhaus are not just cozy, they also offer a great view of the surrounding peaks.

The pleasantly steep approach to the Ramolhaus leads along well—marked trails.

cheese-filled pancakes. If you wish, you can take the trail from the hut toward Ramolferner, or more precisely to the northern Ramolkogel, which reaches about 11,155 feet. Crampons are essential here. The trail gets steeper and steeper up the glacier to the ledge of the right ridge. Here, you can climb to the summit cross, which is adorned by a globe. It reminds hikers of the Tyrolean cartographer Peter Anich, for whom the summit was named. The return to the hut is easy. And then you can look forward to toasting a great day's tour together.

TOURS

TOUR 1 LANGTALERECKHÜTTE
Bridge across the Gurgler Ache gorge to the Langtalereckhütte
» 820 ft/250 m EG   » 3.1 mi/5 km
» 2.5 h   » medium

TOUR 2 HINTERER SPIEGELKOGEL & FIRMISANSCHNEIDE
Tour of 2 10,000-ft peaks with climbing level II passages; descent to Obergurgl
» 2,625 ft/800 m EG   » 7.8 mi/12.5 km
» 5.5 h   » medium

TOUR 3 SCHALFKOGEL
S to the Firmisanjoch; watch out for the crevasses
» 1,968 ft/600 m EG   » 2.5 mi/4 km
» 3 h   » medium

AUSTRIA | TYROL

27

The Dragon's Lair

COBURGER HÜTTE The Coburger Hütte is directly above the dark, beautiful Drachensee. But it isn't the only thing creates a great ambiance; the view across the lake to the mighty Zugspitze inspires guests again and again. The hut certainly enjoys one of the most beautiful locations in the Northern Limestone Alps.

Nestled between the turquoise-blue Seebensee and the no less enchanting Drachensee, the Coburger Hütte enjoys an incomparable view of the shapely peaks of the Mieminger Chain.

We've climbed to the Coburger Hütte countless times. Trails lead across the exciting Hoher Gang or comfortably from the mountain station of the gondola to the Ehrwalder Alm.

Today, we're actually trying something new. Since the Hoher Gang is temporarily closed, we're attempting the Ilmensteig. After an easy start, it ascends steeply across a rocky crest. This terrain requires absolutely dry conditions, otherwise it's all mud. At the top, there is a wide gravel road that leads to the Seebenalm. We climb a bit further uphill, where the first highlight of our hike is waiting for us: The Seebensee. It's just a magical place. This beautiful lake is in the middle of the Mieminger Chain, and the mighty Zugspitze rises in the background.

We walk along the lake and then tackle the steep final climb to the Coburger Hütte. The view gets better with every meter of altitude, and we enjoy the dreamlike landscape.

Once you have finally arrived, the hospitable hut owners Jürgen and Sonja are ready to receive you. They take such tender care of their guests that the stress of the ascent is quickly forgotten.

● AUSTRIA | TYROL | COBURGER HÜTTE

Thanks to the home-style cuisine, hikers can also recharge their batteries. Freshly prepared Tyolian bacon with cheese dumpling soup or an afternoon "Brettljause" (snack) taste excellent. Vegetarian dishes are also available, and if you have a sweet tooth, you can enjoy Kaiserschmarrn with applesauce.

You will sleep well in the bunk beds, which are divided across rooms of various sizes—from quadruple rooms to thirteen-bed dormitories. You must use a hut or linen sleeping bag. But don't worry if you didn't bring one, they won't make you climb back down; sleeping bags are available for sale in the hut.

The hut is equipped with both a shoe room and a drying room, so that even if your climb was rainy, your possessions will dry. One amenity that's rather uncommon in huts is hot showers. The washrooms and toilets were renovated in 2011 and are neatly maintained.

Incidentally, the first hut was built in 1890. Since then, the Coburger Hütte has been expanded several times. During the expansion,

IN BRIEF

VALLEY TOWN Ehrwald

ALTITUDE 6,299 ft/1,920 m above sea level

OPEN June to early October

ACCOMMODATIONS 80-bed dormitory, 6-bed winter room in the cable car station

FOOD good Tyrolean home cooking; special children's menu

GOOD TO KNOW You can ride a bike up to the material cableway. Free internet

172

COBURGER HÜTTE | TYROL | AUSTRIA

The Hoher Gang, which leads from Ehrwald to the Coburger Hütte, requires surefootedness and no fear of heights.

The bright turquoise Seebensee, a natural high mountain lake, provides pleasant refreshment, especially in the summer months.

a combined heat and power plant that runs on vegetable oil was added. And other kinds of environmentally friendly technology are used in the hut. The material and ingredients for cooking, for example, are not flown in, but transported to the hut by a winch cable car.

In addition to the combined heat and power plant, solar panels generate power, and there is a maintenance-free battery array and three bidirectional inverters. The ultimate goal here is to ensure that the hut's power is CO_2-neutral, so that the hikers will be able to enjoy nature in the future as well.

TOURS

TOUR 1 SCHACHTKOPF
Round trip: Biberwierer Scharte → Schachtkopf → former Silberleithe mining area
» 3,018 ft/920 m EG   » 5.3 mi/8.5 km
» 4.5 h   » easy

TOUR 2 HINTERER TAJAKOPF
Easier peak near the Coburger Hütte; but last passage requires experience and courage
» 1,837 ft/560 m EG   » 3.1 mi/5 km
» 3 h   » medium

TOUR 3 SONNENSPITZRUNDE
Begin at the Ehrwalder Almbahn valley station and go around the Ehrwalder Matterhorn; stay at the Coburger Hütte
» 3,444 ft/1,050 m EG   » 3.98 mi/13.5 km
» 7 h   » medium

AUSTRIA | TYROL

28

WINNEBACHSEEHÜTTE The small Winnebachseehütte enjoys an idyllic location on the lake by the same name, and there's a waterfall nearby too. The hut is a popular mountaineering destination in summer and winter. Its grandiose location, the attractiveness of the area, and family-friendly management contribute to this.

As early as 1900, the Frankfurt an der Oder section decided to equip this wonderful water-rich spot in the Sulztal north of Gries with a base for mountaineers. Today, the hut belongs to the Hof section, which took it over in 1954. Since 1955, it has been managed by the Riml family; among other things, they added a new restaurant with panoramic windows during a general renovation.

No matter which way you get to the hut—whether from Gries in the Sulztal or from Winnebach—when you arrive at your destination, it's nice to dangle your tired feet in the cold water of the Winnebachsee before ending the day on the terrace with a view of the gigantic waterfall or in one of the cozy lounges. Don't miss the lovingly prepared dinner, where you can choose between three main dishes, one of which is vegetarian. The hut hosts do their best to take allergies and food intolerances into account—provided you tell them about these when you register. Ingredients such as eggs, bacon, meat, bread, and potatoes come from the Ötztal and Oberland farmers. Depending

The best of the three elements water, earth, and air can be found at the Winnebachseehütte: At an altitude of 7,782 feet, it is perched between jagged peaks on the shore of a clear mountain lake.

AUSTRIA | TYROL | WINNEBACHSEEHÜTTE

on requirements, a refreshing or warming drink is served with the three-course menu.

If you don't fall right into bed after dinner, you can enjoy socializing with other climbers. Here, you'll have trouble choosing your spot: You can sit in the "Frankfurter Stube" with its traditional charm and original paneling or around the cozy stove in the "Hofer Stube." Or would you rather enjoy the spectacular view of the lake and waterfall through the huge panoramic windows of the "waterfall room"?

For the night, you can either stay in one of the three double rooms with bunk beds or in a dormitory room, or you can sleep in one of the three large rooms that sleep up to eight people for an authentic camp feeling. In winter, there is a room with nine to twelve beds for ski tourers. The Winnebachseehütte is particularly popular as a destination and base for hikers, moun-

IN BRIEF

VALLEY TOWN Gries im Sulztal

ALTITUDE 7,782 ft/2,372 m above sea level

OPEN early March to end of April; end of June to end of September

ACCOMMODATIONS 3 dbl rooms, 2 multi-bed rooms (9 beds total); 22-bed dormitory, 10-bed winter room

FOOD Tyrolian home cooking, à la carte lunch, choice of 3 main dishes

GOOD TO KNOW Luggage transport to the hut via material cableway. Via ferrata and climbing gardens are nearby

WINNEBACHSEEHÜTTE | TYROL | AUSTRIA

When you take a short breather, you can't take your eyes off the impressive waterfall.

taineers, climbers, ski tourers, and snowshoe hikers, but there is also a large playground with sand that invites children to dig and swing; blocks around the hut are ideal for gymnastics; and damming up streams has always been great fun. A special experience is the hut's pigs and goats. In the "Kleinkanada" climbing garden, children can take their first steps on vertical rock under their parents' watchful eyes.

TOURS

TOUR 1 ERNST-RIML-SPITZE
Längenfeld parking lot → Winnebachseehütte → Ernst-Riml-Spitze (2,512 m). This tour is suitable for families with children
» 3,051 ft/930 m EG » 6.8 mi/11 km
» 5 h » medium

TOUR 2 SELLRAINER HÜTTENRUNDE
Challenging round trip: 9 stages; beautiful peaks → quiet valleys → hut to hut. High alpine trails: Sellraintal and Ötztal → Inntal. Trail starts and ends in Sellrain
» 34,842 ft/10,620 m EG
» 74.6 mi/120km » 72 h » difficult

You can already see the waterfall, which flows into the Winnebachsee; this means that it's not far to the hut.

🇦🇹 AUSTRIA | TYROL | WINNEBACHSEEHÜTTE

Historical settlement

Water has always held a special attraction for people since it is the elixir of life. Remains of historical fireplaces, dating from 1460 to 1310 BC, were found near the Winnebachseehütte. The area was therefore already settled in the Middle Bronze Age, which was considered the highlight of alpine farming in the Ötztal. However, if you're thinking about the famous man in the ice, known worldwide as "Ötzi," you're way off base because Ötzi, who was discovered by chance in 1991, died much earlier, namely between 3359 and 3105 BC according to calculations and studies. But the place where this "ice mummy" was found is only about 25 miles from the hut as the crow flies.

While the man in the picture is making a pot, two boys collect branches for the fire. This is how everyday life on the Winnebachsee in the Middle Bronze Age might have looked.

WINNEBACHSEEHÜTTE | TYROL | AUSTRIA

AUSTRIA | TYROL

29

The Musical One

SIEGERLANDHÜTTE The Siegerlandhütte is located in the remotest part of the Windachtal in the Stubai Alps. The trail from Sölden is long, but you can also take a taxi bus part of the way. The hut is simple but very cozy. You can end a beautiful mountain day in the small dining room. If you want to make things cozier, you can sing an evening song.

Orange and blue striped shutters adorn the imposing stone building of the Siegerlandhütte at an altitude of 8,891 feet.

If the sky is clear and temperatures are neither too hot nor too cold, you will never be alone on the Sonklarspitze trail on a weekend. After all, it is one of the highest Stubai mountain peaks. If you arrive at the final slope to the hut and meet hikers who are telling you that the hut is full, you may feel a bit insecure. So reserving in advance is crucial here. Because then you can be sure you won't have to turn around and you can enjoy your stay in the hut.

The hut is often chock full, for example when the Günzburg section, which helps watch over the hut, is visiting. The music starts after dinner. Songbooks are unpacked and distributed to anyone who wants one. Everyone is immediately invited to sing along, and so the cheerful or wistful sounds of mountain songs fill the cozy room.

The next day, after an enjoyable evening in the hut, it's time to enjoy the clear morning air. It's still cool, the sun is just rising, but wrapped in a warm jacket, you can enjoy the other-worldly view standing in front of the hut. To the east of us lies the

181

AUSTRIA | TYROL | SIEGERLANDHÜTTE

IN BRIEF

VALLEY TOWN Sölden in the Ötztal

ALTITUDE 8,891 ft/2,710 m above sea level

OPEN early June to end of September

ACCOMMODATIONS 10 beds in dbl rooms, 18 beds in multi-bed rooms 21-bed dormitory

FOOD authentic Tyrolean dishes, delicious cakes, convivial evening atmosphere

GOOD TO KNOW Take 3 days and climb one of the numerous peaks

If you gaze across the Windachtal, you'll see the striking Gaiskogel right away.

large Übeltalferner, framed by the Zuckererhütl, Wilder Pfaff, and Wilder Freiger. You can also see the two huts on the South Tyrolean side, the Müllerhütte and the Becherhaus. The mighty Botzer rises to the south, a seemingly unapproachable summit.

In the midst of this magnificent scenery, the Siegerlandhütte was dedicated in 1930. It's the pride of the Siegerland Alpine Club section. On the section's homepage, you will learn that the members' attachment to the Siegerlandhütte is the association's most valuable asset. Many Siegerländer even call it their home in the high mountains, so it is not surprising that the section's members do a lot of the work on a volunteer basis. But it's not just the Siegerländer who work regularly at the hut; there are almost always Günzburger members as well. The Günzburg section doesn't have its own Alpine Club hut, which is why it helps watch over the Siegerlandhütte. The hut is marked by the volunteers' passion. Because as cozy as the hut is, it's very clean and well-kept. When you return to the hut after a day trip, it's best to enjoy delici-

SIEGERLANDHÜTTE | TYROL | AUSTRIA

ous homemade cake on the sunny bench on the south side. If the weather is bad, there's no reason to worry, for there's a warm, crackling tiled stove in the hut. In the evening, you can look forward to a hearty Tyrolean meal. With all this comfort, it's easy to forget that you're at an altitude of more than 8,858 feet. Power supply here is a challenge—so it's great that the hut was awarded the environmental seal.

TOURS

TOUR 1 SCHEIBLEHNKOGEL
First 3000-m peak for many people; accessible from the Siegerlandhütte and good for a ski tour in the spring
» 1,181 ft/360 m EG   » 1.9 mi/3 km
» 1.5 h   » medium

TOUR 2 SONKLARSPITZE
This ski tour crosses steep terrain; gorgeous descent across the Triebenkarlasferner
» 3,117 ft/950 m EG   » 5.0 mi/8 km
» 4 h   » difficult

TOUR 3 WINDACHTAL HUT TOUR
5-day hike: Brunnenkoglhaus → Siegerlandhütte → Hildesheimer Hütte → Hochstubaihütte
» 13,123 ft/4,000 m EG   » 32.3 mi/52 km
» 18 h   » difficult

The 10,023-foot-high Scheiblehnkogel at the end of the Windachtal is the Siegerlandhütte's local mountain.

183

AUSTRIA | TYROL

30

The Versatile One

FRANZ-SENN-HÜTTE Hiking, mountaineering, high-altitude tours, climbing, via ferrata, ski tours, high–altitude ski tours, and even swimming. There are probably only a few huts in the Eastern Alps that offers as many different activities as the Franz-Senn-Hütte. Families and Alpine Club sections know this, so the hut is very popular.

Finally we are standing at the entrance to the Franz-Senn-Hütte. It's already 9 PM; we have arrived for dinner much later than planned. Actually, ours was a familiar tour, one we have done often with groups. Across the Turmferner to the Vorderer Wilder Turm and over the Turmscharte and the Verborgener-Berg-Ferner back to the hut. Somehow, everything took longer than usual today. But we are looking forward to finally sitting down to a three-course dinner to end the day. At least we made the most of this long summer day.

One of the strengths of the Franz-Senn-Hütte is its location. You can put together a program for the day depending on the weather, your skills, and mood. The climbing gardens and via ferrata around the hut promise fun and adventure. Although it is relatively short, the Edelweiss via ferrata requires skill. Some people have reached their limits here. Even more impressive is the Höllenrachen via ferrata. It leads across a dark gorge directly above the roaring water. If you want to combine a via

The colorful Tibetan prayer flags are meant to remind hikers of the time when Horst Fankhauser—the father of the current hut host and a legendary mountaineer—narrowly escaped with his life in a snowstorm below the Manaslu in 1972.

185

AUSTRIA | TYROL | FRANZ-SENN-HÜTTE

ferrata with a summit experience, you can do this perfectly at the Rinnenspitze, a real 10,000-foot peak. The exposed summit via ferrata is relatively easy, and the panoramic view is magnificent. Next to the impressive ice giants of the Stubai Alps, our view sweeps downward. The blue "eye" of the Rinnensee lies there.

But of course, the Franz-Senn-Hütte is first and foremost a high-altitude hut, even though the glaciers have retreated sharply. Even the mighty Alpeiner Ferner has shrunk by more than 1.5 miles since its peak in 1850. The highest peak in the vicinity is the Ruderhofspitze. However, the climb across the flat glacier is quite long. The Turmschafte and the Innere Sommerwand can be reached more quickly. But here too, glaciers have melted in recent years and there is more and more loose rock. That's why people like to make these tours in early summer.

In addition to the climbing gardens and the via ferrata, there is also a Flying Fox over the

IN BRIEF

VALLEY TOWN Neustift im Stubaital

ALTITUDE 7,043 ft/2,147 m above sea level

OPEN End of February to early May and mid-June to end of September

ACCOMMODATIONS no dbl rooms, 80 beds in shared rooms, 100-bed dormitory, 12-bed winter room

FOOD Tyrolean cuisine with breakfast buffet and evening menu

GOOD TO KNOW Material cableway for luggage transport

FRANZ-SENN-HÜTTE | TYROL | AUSTRIA

If you think that grandma's apple strudel is the best, you should definitely try the tasty treats at the Franz-Senn-Hütte. (top) You'll be there soon—the hut is already within sight! (below)

Gschwetzbach, a true pleasure for both young and old. The hut is also popular in winter. Ski tours to the Wilder Hinterbergl, the Ruderhofspitze, the Innere Sommerwand, or the steep Östliche Seespitze are ski touring classics in the Eastern Alps.

The hut itself is very comfortable, which distinguishes it from other authentic huts in the Alps. It has hot water and free showers, WiFi and cell phone reception. You will be spoiled with a delicious breakfast buffet and a great evening menu.

Power is supplied by a hybrid heating system fueled by electricity, oil, and pyrolysis; waste disposal is done with a semi-biological sewage treatment plant. You can have your luggage brought up by material cableway so that you are well-equipped for several days.

TOURS

TOUR 1 VORDERE SOMMERWAND
Simple climbing route with a rope team
» 1,837 ft/560 m EG   » 1.9 mi/3 km
» 3.5 h   » easy

TOUR 2 INNERE SOMMERWAND
Especially impressive in winter—combine with a ski tour. Franz-Senn-Hütte → Sommerwandferner → Kräulscharte, walk across the rocky ridge (which is partly secured) to the summit
» 4,101 ft/1,250 m EG   » 10.6 mi/17 km
» 4 h   » medium

TOUR 3 APERER TURM
Panoramic and technically easy summit; accessible via the Alpeiner Ferner. There are three rope-secured sections on the way
» 2,690 ft/820 m EG   » 7.5 mi/12 km
» 5 h   » medium

At the summit of the Aperer Turn, you have a unique view of the Alpeinertal.

AUSTRIA | TYROL

31

The Base Camp

NÜRNBERGER HÜTTE The stately Nürnberger Hütte is not only a station on the Stubaier Höhenweg, it's also the base camp for the mighty Wilder Freiger and the Östlicher Feuerstein. These are two really great peaks in the Stubai Alps. Now it's possible to take a grandiose round-trip with the crossing of the Wilder Freiger.

Our backpacks are heavy on this Monday in August. Today two of us set out on the long hut trail from Ranalt via the Bsuchalm to the Nürnberger Hütte. So we're relieved when we reach the old stone building, where we are welcomed warmly by the Siller family and assigned to a cozy double room.

The next day we climb up to the famous Stubai 10,000-foot peak, the Wilder Freiger. Previously, the summit climb required glacier equipment, but today the Grüblferner has retreated so far that you only cross a firn field to reach the top. From here it's not far to the main summit. If you want to keep going, the crossing to the South Tyrol is a good option. The descent down the rocky south ridge to Becher is a pleasure and not particularly difficult.

It's also possible to climb the Östlicher Feuerstein from the Nürnberger Hütte. In contrast to the Freiger, however, there is a glacier on the way to the Feuerstein. The ridge from the Pflerscher Hochjoch to the summit requires caution and a lot of experience, for the terrain is crumbly.

← Everyone knows there's gold at the end of the rainbow. And so it is with the Nürnberger Hütte!

AUSTRIA | TYROL | NÜRNBERGER HÜTTE

IN BRIEF

VALLEY TOWN Ranalt

ALTITUDE 7,473 ft/2,278 m above sea level

OPEN mid-June to early October

ACCOMMODATIONS 2 dbl rooms, 46 beds in shared rooms, 93-bed dormitory

FOOD high-quality and fresh

GOOD TO KNOW Try the climb to the Gamspitzl

On the way from the Nürnberger to the Bremer Hütte, you pass a picturesque small moor, which is rightly called "paradise".

Due to its location, the Nürnberger Hütte is a great base camp for numerous adventures. Actually, this term is usually used for a practical, less comfortable camp far from any form of infrastructure. However, that's not the case with the Nürnberger Hütte: The hut is cozy, friendly, and it serves excellent food. There are even hot showers, which you pay for by the minute.

The friendly hosts Martina and Leonhart Siller procure nearly all the food from their own organic farm in the valley; there's milk, butter, cheese, fruit and vegetables, and all kinds of meat. And you can taste the difference. Rarely is such wonderful food served in a mountain hut. In addition, the hut team likes to supplement the culinary delicacies with Prosecco, which they mix with homemade almrose syrup. In the evening, someone often sings a song, for the Siller family's team is very musical.

If you then retire to the comfortable beds, you're guaranteed to fall asleep in a good mood—you'll be well fortified. The next morning, however, you'll be hungry again. But you can fill

NÜRNBERGER HÜTTE | TYROL | AUSTRIA

up thanks to the ample breakfast buffet. Life won't be boring at the Nürnberger Hütte, for there is a small practice via ferrata that leads to a beautiful rocky viewpoint, plus a great climbing garden. Both are also suitable for children taking their first steps on steep rock. In addition, in bad weather, children can let off some steam in the indoor climbing room. There's even a ping pong table. So it's no wonder why the Alpine Association included the Nürnberger Hütte in its "Take your children to the huts" campaign.

TOURS

TOUR 1 MAIRSPITZE
Experienced hikers can enjoy the Stubai; no special technical difficulties
» 1,542 ft/470 m EG » 1.2 mi/2 km
» 1.5 h » medium

TOUR 2 SULZENAU HÜTTE
Green mountains, mountain lakes, and giant white glaciers
» 1,083 ft/330 m EG » 3.2 mi/5 km
» 2.5 h » difficult

TOUR 3 BREMER HÜTTE
The 6th stage of the Stubaier Höhenweg runs across glaciers and the "Paradise" high moor to the Bremer Hütte
» 1,969 ft/600 m EG » 3.7 mi/6 km
» 4 h » difficult

A stage of the Stubaier Höhenweg runs right along the shore of the turquoise Grünausee.

191

AUSTRIA | TYROL

32

Climbing History

FALKENHÜTTE The Falkenhütte occupies a green space in the shadow of the mighty Laliderer Wände in the northern Karwendel Mountains. Many years of adventurous climbing stories have been written here. Even if those times are long gone, you will still stand awestruck under these impressive rock faces.

If you listen to Horst Wels, the longtime host of the Falkenhütte, who is over 80 years old, you will be infected by his enthusiasm for the mountains. Horst has accomplished many alpine feats in his life, such as the first winter ascent of the Wettersteingrat. He likes to talk about the Laliderer Wände, the impressive rock faces above the Falkenhütte. They are certainly some of the most beautiful rock faces in the Karwendel Mountains. Particularly well-known is the Herzogkante, which leads straight up toward the sky. People are still climbing it today. Nobody climbs the other routes on the walls anymore. Climbing has changed too much for that; people prefer climbing gardens and well-secured plaisir routes. Today, adventure is no longer so much in demand. Things used to be different. The first ascent of the impressive walls and the Herzogkante was made in 1911. Horst Wels was also on the road in this area for many years. His great love, however, is the Laliderer Wände. Later, he became a hut host at the Falkenhütte.

In his honor, the outbuilding was renamed Horst-Wels-Haus. The hut's cornerstone was

The bright blue of the cloudless sky, ocher-colored rocks, and yellow flowers in the lush green meadow—there's no shortage of bright colors around the Falkenhütte.

193

AUSTRIA | TYROL | FALKENHÜTTE

IN BRIEF

VALLEY TOWN Hinterriss

ALTITUDE 6,062 ft/1,848 m above sea level

OPEN early June to October

ACCOMMODATIONS 60 beds in shared rooms, 10 beds in dbl rooms, 60-bed dormitory, 8-bed winter room

FOOD selected regional delicacies

GOOD TO KNOW Bike through the Johannistal to the hut. This does not even require an e-bike. There is free drinking water for refilling your bottles

laid in 1921. Since then, it has stood in the green pastures, which provide a wonderful contrast to its gloomy walls.

Renovation of the hut began in 2017 and it became "the most beautiful construction site in the world." However, this also ended the era of the Kostzer family, who had been hosting the hut since 1947. During the renovation, the lounge, which is a protected historic site, was restored in loving detail. Of particular note are the historic clock, the sideboard, and the bay window. The Horst-Wels-Haus was even completely demolished and rebuilt elsewhere. The hut opened its doors again in August 2020 under the new hosts Claudia and Bertl.

If the climbers don't come, who will use the hut? First and foremost, there are two groups of people. On the one hand, the mountain bikers, as both the Johannistal and the Laliderertal are ideal for biking. You pedal uphill through a valley and treat yourself to a refreshment at the

FALKENHÜTTE | TYROL | AUSTRIA

The almost vertical rock faces of the Laliderer Wände attract more than just ambitious climbers.

Falkenhütte. After that, you rush back through the other valley. Special attention should be paid to the Kleine Ahornboden at the end of the Johannistal. This gem is much more beautiful and tranquil than its big brother in the Eng.

The second group is hikers. After all, the famous Karwendel Tour leads from Scharnitz to Pertisau via the Falkenhütte. Depending on how you plan the hike, you can stay overnight in the hut. Then you can enjoy the night in the new eco-friendly bed linen.

But the hut is also good for a day trip. You hike the whole way under the imposing walls, so you can let your imagination can run wild.

TOURS

TOUR 1 MAHNKOPF
A short hike to the grassy summit
» 1,148 ft/350 m EG   » 1.1 mi/1.8 km
» 1 h   » easy

TOUR 2 GAMSJOCH
Long ascent; magnificent view of the Karwendel main chain up to the Birkkarspitze
» 3,166 ft/965 m EG   » 4.3 mi/7 km
» 3.5 h   » medium

TOUR 3 KARWENDEL TOUR
4-day tour: A dream for alpine connoisseurs. The Lamsenjochhütte and the Eng and Gramai alpine inns offer refreshments
» 14,764 ft/4,500 HM   » 32.3 mi/52 km
» 20 h   » medium

Sunrise plunges the Karwendel main ridge into a beautiful dawn.

195

🇦🇹 AUSTRIA | TYROL | FALKENHÜTTE

70 years of the hut hosts' family

The Kostenzer family was associated with the hut's history for more than 70 years; its members spent their summers in the hut. In 1946, Tilli and Peter Kostenzer took over as hut hosts. Tilli died young, at 44, and Peter continued by himself, with his five children. His son Fritz replaced him at the age of 20. Actually, the intention was that one of his sisters should take over. But she got married, so Fritz stayed in the hut. He quickly realized that it was his calling to host guests in his high-altitude home. He and his wife Ursula hosted the Falkenhütte until 2017, when it was time to renovate. In recent years, they have been actively assisted by their sons. Now Fritz is retiring and the Falkenhütte has been operated by a new couple of hosts since its reopening in 2020.

A look at the hut's album provides impressions of the past: It all began in 1921, when the first stone was laid (picture above right).

196

FALKENHÜTTE | TYROL | AUSTRIA

197

AUSTRIA | TYROL

The Cozy One

GAMSHÜTTE The small Gamshütte in the Zillertal is a particularly cozy hut. Some of the beds are located outside in a smaller auxiliary hut. Its panoramic position below the Grinbergspitze high above the most remote part of the Zillertal is sensational. This hut is an optimal starting point for the popular Berliner Höhenweg.

The Gamshütte is a place to which you will inevitably return again and again, because once you've been there, this little hut will remain close to your heart.

For many years it belonged to the large Berlin section of the German Alpine Club. In 1993 it was acquired by the small Bavarian Otterfing section. This was followed by a comprehensive renovation of the hut with installation of solar panels and the construction of a washroom. Today, almost 30 years later, the hut is again being adapted to current requirements. However, it should continue to be the cozy hut we have come to know and love. Above all, new staff rooms will be created and the kitchen converted to use more modern energy sources. The outdoor shower with spring water will remain. It's not just popular because it's so refreshing; it's practical, but it also offers a fantastic view of the Dristner and the Floitental. There's also a wonderful view from the terrace, but here you can see the Zillertal with the Penken and Rastkogel and further to the Tux Alps. Corinna Epp hosts the hut lovingly and with great

← Only the view from above illustrates the fantastic location of the Gamshütte. From the terrace, there's a great view of the Zillertal.

AUSTRIA | TYROL | GAMSHÜTTE

IN BRIEF

VALLEY TOWN Finkenberg

ALTITUDE 6,302 ft/1,921 m above sea level

OPEN mid-June to end of September

ACCOMMODATIONS 38-bed dormitory

FOOD very tasty dishes with soups, home-baked bread, hut classics, and the regional speciality "Zillertal lumberjack donuts"

GOOD TO KNOW No warm water; showers are outdoors

The high, green valley where the town of Finkenberg is located rises gently to the imposing mountains of Mayrhofen.

commitment. This former bookseller from Munich worked in other huts for many summers and finally fulfilled her dream of hosting her own hut. She and her motivated team, which consists primarily of women, take excellent care of the guests.

Corinna emphasizes regional ingredients for her small but fine selection of dishes. The Gamshütte was awarded the DAV seal "This is how the mountains taste." This means that the ingredients usually come from sources within about 30 miles of the hut. She prepares various daily dishes, soups, and snacks. Since Corinna started hosting it, the hut has enjoyed an excellent culinary reputation among its guests and it is also very popular with locals. In her first year, she set a new record with just over 2,000 overnight stays.

In addition to the many day visitors, it's mainly hut hikers who come to the Gamshütte. The Gamshütte offers the first overnight accommodation on the popular Berliner Höhenweg. There's a nice, friendly reception in the Zillertal.

GAMSHÜTTE | TYROL | AUSTRIA

The next morning, you'll set out refreshed on the first long stage. After a long eight-hour hike, you will reach the Friesenberghaus, which still belongs to the Berlin Alpine Club section. This is how you can set out directly on the Berliner Höhenweg. The second stage is one of the longest stages of this high-altitude trail. Once you have completed it, you will certainly be well-equipped for the other sections of the trail.

The Hermann-Hecht-Weg is the best way to ascend to the hut. It is very shady, and the upper part of the ascent takes you through the Ebenschlag natural forest reserve. There has been no human intervention in the forest for over 20 years, so this feels like a hike through a magical fairy-tale forest.

Again and again, cows cross hikers' paths. Even if they seem cuddly, these animals should be treated with respect and appropriate caution.

TOURS

TOUR 2 GRINBERGSPITZE
This classic tour ends at the Vordere Grinbergspitze. Crossing to the second summit takes 30 minutes on unmarked trails with some easy climbing. The ascent to the Hinterespitze requires 3rd degree climbing and another 30 minutes
» 2,789 ft/850 m EG   » 5.5 km
» 4 h   » medium

TOUR 3 FRIESENBERGHAUS
2nd stage of the Berliner Höhenweg: Longest and least populated. Nearly all of the trail is at an altitude of 2,000 meters
» 3,806 ft/1,160 m EG   » 14 km   » 8 h
» difficult

201

HUT BOOK

HUT BOOK

Hut guidebook: There's no sinful behavior at the hut...right? Mountaineering rules

There are a few rules that you should be sure to follow in alpine huts. These include making a reservation and canceling it should your plans change. After you arrive, you register with the host and put your hut sleeping bag in the sleeping quarters. People like to eat and drink in huts, and the hosts need to make a living too. You should use water sparingly; don't take long showers. Frequently, there are separate washrooms for men and women. Of course you should adapt your behavior to the conditions. Even if the sleeping quarters are sometimes very cozy, the hut isn't a place for "sinful behavior." Unless you're all by yourselves in a small self-catering hut...

No one will object to a goodnight kiss before going to bed.

AUSTRIA | TYROL

The Alpine Castle

BERLINER HÜTTE The Berliner Hütte is listed as a historic monument; it is the only Alpine Association hut to have earned this honor. You open the heavy wooden door and are amazed at the huge chandelier. And really you're not entering a hut, but an "Alpine Castle," as the Berliner Hütte is also called. The dining room is also magnificent. In the Alpine Castle, you could almost forget that you're in the high mountains.

While the high ceilings make the dining room of the Berliner Hütte appear pompous and magnificent, the rustic wood paneling provides a cozy flair.

When we were at the Berliner Hütte for the first time, we were disappointed to find that it was quite crowded. We'd carried our heavy backpacks all the way through the Zemmgrund for this? We lay in the winter room hoping that the night would pass quickly. We weren't even enthusiastic about the ski tour on the Ochsner because of the dense fog and poor snow quality. Perhaps it wasn't the best idea to spend Easter at the Berliner Hütte. In addition, its characteristic "Alpine Castle" flair was not on display, because the main building is closed in winter. Things look quite different a few years later. We take a relaxed hike on the forest path through the Zemmgrund in sneakers. Our backpacks are heavy again, but that doesn't bother us today. The sun is shining, and so we reach the Berliner Hütte in a good mood. When we enter the entrance hall, we're speechless. A mighty chandelier hangs from the ceiling and gives us an idea of the significance

AUSTRIA | TYROL | BERLINER HÜTTE

of the hut for the Berlin Alpine Club when it was built in 1879. Later we enter the dining room where we will eat our dinner, and we can hardly believe that we are in the high mountains. Both of these rooms are extraordinarily sumptuously furnished. It's nice that this is still the case decades later. Meanwhile, the Berliner Hütte is the only Alpine Association hut that is listed as a historic monument. It's also impressive that it's had electricity since 1910. This hut was also the first one to have a hydroelectric power plant.

In the mornings, it's initially very quiet at the Berliner Hütte. This way, you can enjoy the dining room in peace—and the delicious food that the hut hosts Maike and Florian prepare themselves. They know precisely what hikers need to "tank up" on energy for the day, especially if a tour to the summit of the Schwarzenstein is on the agenda. In recent years, the glacier there has retreated a lot, as have many others. The Hornkees, for example, shrank by 340 feet in 2020 alone, setting a sad record for Austria's glaciers. Accordingly, there are not many guests in the Berliner Hütte who undertake high-altitude tours from there. But the hike over the Schwarzensteinkees to the summit cross on this mighty almost 10,000-foot peak on the border with South Tyrol is all the more beautiful when you share the path—and the view at the end—with other people. The hustle

IN BRIEF

VALLEY TOWN Ginzling

ALTITUDE 6,699 ft/2,042 m above sea level

OPEN mid-June to end of September

ACCOMMODATIONS 75 beds, 102-bed dormitory, 14-bed winter room

FOOD Breakfast buffet and half board; good, down-to-earth Tyrolean food

GOOD TO KNOW Very long gravel road through the Zemmgrund; wear sneakers. In high season, be sure to book ahead to get a room

BERLINER HÜTTE | TYROL | AUSTRIA

The friendly front desk not only welcomes guests, but also helps them with any questions they may have. (top)

In order to stay in such a cozy single room, you must book well in advance. (below)

and bustle at breakfast at the Berliner Hütte only begins later when the "Höhenweg hikers" appear. The Berliner Höhenweg, which takes you from hut to hut, is the driving force in the Zillertal. Of course, the highlight is the oldest hut on the Höhenweg, the Berliner Hütte.

But if you don't want to go so high, you can also stay close to the hut and simply enjoy the sun and the view. Or take a short detour to the romantic Schwarzsee. After that, it's time to say goodbye to the "Alpine Castle" and take your memories and impressions back down into the valley. ✻

TOURS

TOUR 1 SCHÖNBICHLER HORN
Exposed before the summit –hikers must be surefooted and courageous. A via ferrata set is useful
» 4,396 ft/1,340 m EG » 5 km
» 3.5 h » easy

TOUR 2 ZSIGMONDYSPITZE
Ascent to the "Zillertaler Matterhorn"; popular climb in the Zillertal Alps. Climbing experience required
» 3,871 ft/1,180 m EG » 5 km
» 3.5 h » medium

TOUR 3 GROSSER MÖRCHNER
Challenging tour on the Grosser Mörchner: glacier equipment and experience essential
» 4,068 ft/1,240 m EG » 6 km
» 4 h » difficult

On the descent from the Schönbichler Horn back to the Berliner Hütte, these two hikers have a great view of the Schwarzensteinkees.

207

AUSTRIA | TYROL

35

The Pearl

← Above the clouds...the freedom at the Greizer Hütte knows no bounds. The magnificent view of the Floitengrund, Felsköpfl, and Triebbachkopf underscores this statement.

GREIZER HÜTTE Family–friendly and a starting point for high alpine tours: Its location in the beautiful remotest part of the Zillertal, near the Flotienkees, makes the Greizer Hütte a connection between two worlds. Anyone who arrives here is either just starting or finishing. In both cases, however, hikers have reached a unique place full of rustic coziness, which is rightly called the pearl of the Berliner Höhenweg.

We're sitting back at the Greizer Hütte, slowly recovering from the shock. We were on the Großer Löffler, one of the grandiose Zillertal almost 10,000-foot peaks. The climb was challenging. The glacier is quite steep and did not have particularly good snow cover. In some places, we had to secure ourselves. Up to that point, everything had gone well. We enjoyed the exciting ascent and reached the summit. And our descent across the steep Floitenkees presented no problems. But then, at the end of the glacier when we were pulling off our crampons, there was suddenly falling rock. Luckily it missed us, but we were scared; we didn't really recover until we reached the hut.

Fortunately, the Greizer Hütte can calm your mind quickly with its cozy charm. It is hosted by Herbert and Irmi. These two keep their calm even when the hut is very busy—and this happens pretty often. Located direcly

AUSTRIA | TYROL | GREIZER HÜTTE

The Greizer Hütte is simple but very cozy.

On the way back from the Mörchnerscharte to the Greizer Hütte, hike along the Berliner Höhenweg and enjoy a wonderful view of the Greizer and the Lappenspitze.

on the Berliner Höhenweg, many hikers' tours end right here, at the Greizer Hütte, with the descent through the Floitengrund. With its cozy flair and friendly hosts, the hut is the ideal place to conclude a great multi-day tour on the Berliner Höhenweg.

The Greizer Hütte has been in the Floitengrund since 1893. The history of the Greiz section has been characterized by some ups and downs. The section was founded in 1880 in Greiz, southern Thuringia. When the hut was built, the section had only 116 members, but thanks to their collective efforts and commitment, they managed to construct the hut. After the Second World War, the section was initially dissolved by the Allies, but it was re-founded in 1955 by people originally from Greiz in honor of their homeland, but in West Germany, in Marktredwitz. And the Greizer Hütte was soon returned to its section.

To this day, many hut guests arrive here via the Berliner Höhenweg. Alternatively, a path leads across the Floitengrund. From here, routes such as the one on the Großer Löffler

IN BRIEF

VALLEY TOWN Ginzling

ALTITUDE 7,306 ft/2,227 m above sea level

OPEN mid-June to early October

ÜBERNACHTEN 2 double rooms, 20 beds in multi-bed rooms, 58-bed dormitory, 14-bed winter room

FOOD Tyrolean cuisine; hot chocolate with milk from the hut's goats is served on request

GOOD TO KNOW Make the climb shorter with a taxi and luggage transport by material cableway

GREIZER HÜTTE | TYROL | AUSTRIA

and the Schwarzenstein beckon as tour destinations; these routes are much more challenging from this side than from the Berliner Hütte.

If you want to climb an easier summit, try the Gigalitz. You can reach this nearly 10,000-foot summit on a marked rocky path in two hours. No matter where you come from: A stay at the Greizer Hütte is always a special experience. The hut team will spoil you with seasonal culinary delicacies such as blueberry pancakes, roast chamois, or chanterelles. In addition to the tasty food, hammocks and deck chairs on the sun terrace make you want to sit back and relax for a change. And the hut is environmentally conscious as well. Power supplied by the small hydropower system and solar panels are part of this, as is the hut's no-waste policy. That's why it received the Alpine Association's environmental seal of approval in 2005.

TOURS

TOUR 1 ASCENT FROM GINZLING
Easy trail: Tristenbachalm → Wirtshaus Steinbock and valley station of the material cableway to the Greizer Hütte
» 4,035 ft/1,230 m EG » 6.2 mi/10 km
» 4.5 h » easy

TOUR 2 KASSELER HÜTTE
Across the Lapenscharte and the Löfflerkar, hikers on the Berliner Höhenweg are literally on the ropes
» 2,460 ft/750 m EG » 5.9 mi/9.5 km
» 6 h » medium

TOUR 3 GROSSER LÖFFLER
Glacier tour over the Floitenkees; quite difficult. Get a mountain guide!
» 3,937 ft/1,200 m EG » 4.3 mi/7 km
» 4 h » difficult

Hikers have to cross a suspension bridge at the transition to the Kasseler Hütte.

AUSTRIA | TYROL | GREIZER HÜTTE

In "Marmot Land"

Alpine marmots are truly in paradise in the Floitengrund. There's plenty of alpine grass to eat, and the area's deep soil provides plenty of room for their burrows. They withdraw to their burrows when it's hot or if they're in danger. They also spend the winter there—sleeping. Their digestive systems slow down to a minimum, and their breathing and heartbeat slow to save energy. When hibernating, they take only two breaths a minute and their hearts beat just 20 times. Only when the outside temperature is high enough do the marmots wake up from their deep sleep, which lasts between six and seven months—and sometimes even nine months. Then it's possible that you'll cross these animals' paths—or at least hear their whistles.

→

The marmots' characteristic whistle is actually a warning call. The animals alert each other as soon as enemies such as foxes or golden eagles appear.

GREIZER HÜTTE | TYROL | AUSTRIA

AUSTRIA | TYROL

The Bear Hut

Both bears—at least if you believe the stories—and donkeys seem to like the Anton-Karg-Hütte. Not to mention the many climbers.

ANTON-KARG-HAUS Nestled between the Wilder and Zahmer Kaier, the Anton-Karg-Haus is located in the remotest part of the Kaisertal under the Kleiner Halt. The hut is named after the former section chair of the Austrian Alpine Association, Kufstein section. It's also known by its old name, Hinterbärenbad. It is said that brown bears used to bathe in the Kaiserbach on hot summer days exactly where the hut stands today.

How cozy, how idyllic: This dark wood mountain hut with its green shutters is the epitome of a family-friendly destination. Even the trail here through the charming landscape of the Kaiser Mountains is pure relaxation. The refuge itself, in the remotest part of the Kaisertal, is framed by densely overgrown slopes and surrounded by firs. It has been here since 1883. It was built by the Kufstein section of the German Alpine Club, which rebuilt a former alpine hut and opened it under the name Hinterbärenbadhütte. Over the years, it was constantly expanded and became a popular excursion destination for the Kufsteiner. Balconies were even added to some rooms. The hut is named after Anton Karg, who served as the hut's host starting in 1888. He was also the first chair of the Kufstein Alpine Club section from 1890 to 1919. The hut's original name came from the point on the Kaiserbach where it is said that bears swam in the past. However, the bears probably just liked to look

AUSTRIA | TYROL | ANTON-KARG-HAUS

for food here. Unfortunately, this almost led to their extinction: Out of concern for their livestock, the region's farmers hunted the bears relentlessly. Luckily, now people in Austria are aware of the important role that bears play in the sensitive ecosystem of the Alps. On the so-called Bärenweg, which starts at the Anton-Karg-Haus, children and adults learn interesting facts about bears as they hike along the foot of the Wilder Kaiser.

But the hut is more than just an ideal starting point for pleasure hikers. From here, people with sporting ambitions can take many climbing tours in the mountains of the Wilder Kaiser—one of the most famous climbing destinations in Austria. Whether you tackle the classic Kaiserschützensteig on the Ellmauer Halt, the challenging Kufsteiner via ferrata, or the "climbing secret" pleasure climbing tour on

IN BRIEF

VALLEY TOWN Kufstein

ALTITUDE 2,720 ft/829 m above sea level

OPEN early May to end of October, depending on the snow conditions

ACCOMMODATIONS 35 beds in dbl and quad rooms, 67 beds in shared rooms, no classic dormitory

FOOD exceptionally good food; classic Brettljausen, pressed cheese dumplings, and homemade cakes

GOOD TO KNOW Playground and treehouse for children; defined pool in the Kaiserbach

ANTON-KARG-HAUS | TYROL | AUSTRIA

The Kleine Halt is next to the Totenkirchl, the showpiece of the Kaisertal. Surely it doesn't hurt to visit the chapel before a climbing tour.

Guided tours called "The Kaiser's Herbal Treasures" are offered in the Kaisertal.

the Kleiner Halt, it's up to each climber to choose his or her own adventure. If you still haven't had enough, you can let off some steam in the hut's bouldering room.

Staying overnight in the Anton-Karg-Haus is akin to staying in a comfortable youth hostel. Guests can choose between twin, four and six-bed rooms, with or without bunk beds. Should it be uncomfortable outside, the large, dark-wood paneled lounge attracts people with its hearty tavern atmosphere. Spending cozy evenings with games, fun, and good food is practically mandatory here. The hosts Dagmar and Alexander Egger take care of the latter and spoil their guests with regional specialties. The menu ranges from the "Brettljause" (snack) to pressed cheese dumplings to homemade cakes and tarts. Freshly fortified, you can explore the surrounding area, which offers something for everyone, with several possibilities for climbing the summit. ✹

TOURS

TOUR 1 STRIPSENJOCHHAUS
Trail below the Kleiner Halt and Totenkirchl → beautiful hut in the Kaisergebirge
» 2,329 ft/710 m EG   » 2.5 mi/4 km
» 2.5 h   » easy

TOUR 2 SONNECK
Trail 97 → Karl-Güttler-Steig → Gamskar; cross rocky area to the summit
» 4,396 ft/1,340 m EG   » 3.7 mi/6 km
» 4 h   » medium

TOUR 3 KAISERSCHÜTZENSTEIG
Long, technically challenging, exposed via ferrata via Kleine Halt, Gamshalt, & Ellmauer Halt
» 4,593 ft/1,400 m EG   » 3.7 mi/6 km
» 5.5 h   » difficult

AUSTRIA | TYROL

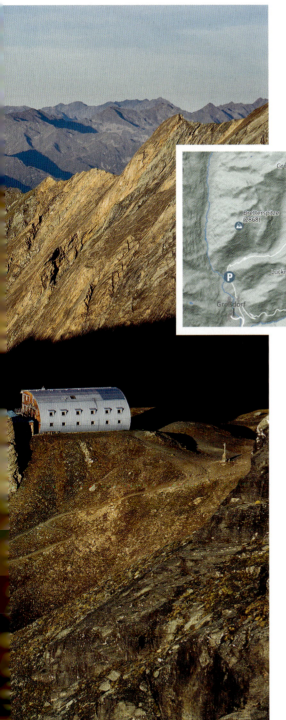

With its long, barrel—shaped new building, architect Albin Glaser's design is tailored to the prevailing wind speeds of over 200 km/h on the Großglockner.

For the King

STÜDLHÜTTE The Großglockner is Austria's highest mountain and one of the most sought-after destinations in the Eastern Alps due to its height and striking shape. The Stüdlhütte is located on the south side of this mighty mountain and has become one of the most important bases for a Glockner ascent. The impressive Stüdlgrat route is particularly popular from this hut.

It's late when we arrive at the hut. It's May, and we want to ski on the "king" of Austria. Up above, we're surprised by the warm hospitality and great dinner buffet. It's relatively quiet in the hut, we deliberately chose to hike during the week. That's also the key to enjoying the Stüdlhütte. On weekends, the Großglockner is regularly overcrowded.

The first hut was built on the Fanatscharte early on. Johann Stüdl, a merchant from Prague, organized and financed construction of the first hut in 1867. This created an opportunity to climb the Großglockner from the Kalser side. It was also the German Alpine Club's first hut. The small Prague section continued to exist in West Germany after the Second World War, then in the 1990s it became part of the Oberland section. The old hut was so dilapidated that it was replaced by a completely new building in 1996.

As soon as you arrive, you'll notice the building's special shape. It's a trimmed ellipse, and the aluminum roof is pulled to the ground on

AUSTRIA | TYROL | STÜDLHÜTTE

the windward side. That's how it stands up to the gusts. The building is almost completely self-sufficient in terms of energy. This was truly special when it was built, and a new evolutionary stage in hut construction. However, the new building cost the Oberland section quite a lot of energy, not to mention money.

Today, about 25 years later, there's still a comfortable, cozy shelter here. However, its location is threatened by the thawing permafrost. The slope below the hut is thawing more and more due to climate change, so in the future, slope preservation measures may be required to save this great alpine location.

The hut itself is managed by the young hosts Matteo and Veronika, who had already gained experience in another large hut in the Hohe Tauern. And that's hard work! In just one season, 15,000 dumplings are rolled, 5,500 servings of

IN BRIEF

VALLEY TOWN Kals am Großglockner

ALTITUDE 9,193 ft/2,802 m above sea level

OPEN Early March to mid-May and mid-June to mid-October

ACCOMMODATIONS no dbl or multi-bed rooms, 122-bed dormitory, 16-bed winter room

FOOD delicious food; generous evening buffet

GOOD TO KNOW Very popular on summer weekends, more relaxed during the week. Hut generates most of its own energy. Card payment possible

STÜDLHÜTTE | TYROL | AUSTRIA

The Pasterze on the Kaiser-Franz-Josefs-Höhe, at more than 8 km in length, is Austria's largest glacier.

Mountaineers on their way to the largest and most famous summit in Austria—the Großglockner.

goulash soup are served, and about 25 pounds of home-baked bread are needed every day.

But it would be a pity to describe the Stüdlhütte only as a base for the Großglockner. A day trip to this impressive hut, which offers an impressive view of the "king's," is a worthwhile undertaking. This hut hike is suitable for getting a close-up view of the high mountains without exposing yourself to great dangers. Nevertheless, you can feel the "king" breath and perhaps develop a desire to climb, using the Stüdlhütte as a base camp. ✸

TOURS

TOUR 1 & 2 SCHERE & FANATKOGEL
Sure-footed hikers can reach both summits: It takes 30 minutes to get to the Schere via a steep cliff; the Fanatkogel is just 15 minutes away via a trail behind the hut
» 721 ft/220 m EG/328 ft/100 m EG
» 30/15 min » easy

TOUR 3 GROSSGLOCKNER
Alpine ski tour: requires extreme caution; risk of crevasses on the glacier and falling on the ridge to the summit. Mandatory: ski touring equipment, crampons, pick, rope, helmet, ice screws, HMS, climbing harness
» 3,280 ft/1,000 m EG » 4 mi/6.4 km
» 5 h » difficult

221

AUSTRIA | TYROL | STÜDLHÜTTE

A High-Ranking Visitor

Friedrich August III, the last king of Saxony, was an enthusiastic alpinist.

The Großglockner has always been a great attraction. In the Stüdlhütte, there is a historic picture of a man in a tourist suit holding an alpenstock. The picture is of King Friedrich August of Saxony, who climbed the Großglockner on August 2, 1910. He was very pleased by the hospitality offered to him at the Stüdlhütte, which is why he presented the owners with the photo in question. So a king visited another "king." This probably wouldn't happen today. However, the mountain "king" will certainly see more visitors today than it did in 1910.

The Großglockner and the Erzherzog-Johann-Hütte, which stands on the rocks of the Adlersruhe directly at the summit, are illuminated by the morning sun.

STÜDLHÜTTE | TYROL | AUSTRIA

AUSTRIA | CARINTHIA

38

The Eldest One

SALMHÜTTE The first Salmhütte near the Großglockner was built in 1799. People wanted to climb Austria's highest mountain, and for that they needed a base; that was the Salmhütte. That's how it became the first hut in the Eastern Alps. Visitors can immediately sense this friendly hut's long history. Its proximity to the Großglockner makes climbers' hearts leap.

Finally we arrived at the small Salmhütte at the southern foot of the steep Schwerteck. We're feeling a little disappointed and exhausted. Disappointed because we have not managed to reach our goal of standing at the summit of the Großglockner. There were simply too many people on the Kleinglockner's narrow ridge. Rope teams that were completely chaotic, and thus also posed a danger to others. In addition, there were "traffic jams" in the notch right before the main summit. So with heavy hearts, we decided not to climb the last few feet.

We're exhausted because it was a long day. We started early at the Stüdlhütte and climbed over the Ködnitzkees to the Adlersruhe and on in the direction of the Glockner. But we did not just want to check the "mountain" box; we wanted a more intensive mountain experience. That's why we chose the descent via the Salmhütte, where we planned an additional night. And it was worth it. It feels different here than at the summit. There is no hectic hustle and bustle. We can enjoy nature in peace here. Quickly, our disappointment

The Salmhütte is shrouded in fog, while the sun is already shining on the lonely Schober group in the background.

225

AUSTRIA | CARINTHIA | SALMHÜTTE

IN BRIEF

VALLEY TOWN Kals am Großglockner, Kaiser-Franz-Josefs-Höhe, and Heiligenblut

ALTITUDE 8,675 ft/2,644 m above sea level

OPEN mid-June to end of September

ACCOMMODATIONS 28 beds in multi-bed rooms, 22-bed dormitory, 6-bed winter room, no dbl rooms

FOOD Austrian cuisine

GOOD TO KNOW The quiet side of the Großglockner. The Wiener Höhenweg is an interesting stage tour. Cash payment only

The age of ibex can be determined by the ring-shaped recesses of their horns.

turns into pure joy about the gift of being allowed to be here, because we decided against the usual procedure of climbing the Glockner in two days. The additional day was an excellent idea, for it's the perfect tonic for our hectic everyday lives. So sitting on the terrace enjoying the warm rays of the afternoon sun, we can look up at the king of the Eastern Alps, our former destination.

It's hard to believe that the first base for a Glockner ascent was all the way up here. Today, the Salmhütte isn't the main Glockner base. The climb from the Stüdlhütte to the Lucknerhaus is too direct. Even the Wiener Höhenweg, which leads through the Schober Group to the Salmhütte, doesn't draw that many people. The Schober group is just not famous enough. But perhaps this territory is worth exploring too, because the quiet moments in the mountains are the most precious.

Today's Salmhütte has nothing in common with the first hut. It was quickly destroyed. The foundation for the current hut dates from 1926/27. It was already the third Salmhütte. It was not until 2017 that the hut was extended and the kitchen greatly improved. By expanding

SALMHÜTTE | CARINTHIA | AUSTRIA

Since the day of the first ascent of the Großglockner—July 28, 1800—there has been a cross at the summit.

the kitchen, the range of dishes could be increased a great deal. The hut's host, Helga, can now spoil you with Austrian specialties and large portions. In the evening, you snuggle up in cozy beds before you start your journey the next morning, after a delicious breakfast.

On the descent, we think back on what we've experienced. We notice how our feelings have changed due to the contrast between hectic and calm. We would like to return to this marvelous region. And not just to try the Großglockner again. Because the big name is certainly a draw, but now we feel peaceful and relaxed.

TOURS

TOUR 1 ERZHERZOG-JOHANN-HÜTTE
Ascent follows the trail of the first people to climb the Großglockner across the Hohenwartscharte
» 3,117 ft/950 m EG   » 2.5 mi/4 km
» 3.5 h   » medium

TOUR 2 WIENER HÖHENWEG
6 stages: Multi-day hike through the Schober Group passes 7 huts
» 11,483 ft/3,500 m EG   » 25 mi/40 km
» 23 h   » difficult

TOUR 3 GLOCKNERRUNDE
The Glocknerrunde takes you from hut to hut in 7 days. Expect to hike 3 to 8 hours a day
» 23,294 ft/7,100 m EG   » 60 mi/95 km
» 44 h   » difficult

AUSTRIA | CARINTHIA | SALMHÜTTE

The first ascent of the Großglockner

No one had been up there yet, on Austria's highest mountain. So somebody had to go! So the Carinthian Archbishop Franz Xaver Graf von Salm-Reifferscheidt took the matter into his hands. First, he needed a base for the ascent, and so the Salmhütte was built at an altitude of 8,740 feet. The first expedition failed; it had to be aborted due to heavy snowfall. But then on July 28, 1800, it was finally time: 62 expedition participants tackled the summit. The much smaller summit troop made it to the Kleinglockner; from there, only the four farmers and carpenters, the leaders of the group, initially climbed up to the summit. They secured the ascent and returned to guide the pastor to the summit. He refused because he was afraid, but the four leaders did not give up and finally persuaded him to come along. For the expedition would only be considered successful if a "gentleman" stood on the summit. But that's not all: The four leaders brought the first summit cross and put their own "crown" on the "king."

Since the first ascent of the Großglockner by Franz Xaver Graf von Salm-Reifferscheidt (left), the summit has become a popular destination—even though it's definitely not for beginners.

228

SALMHÜTTE | CARINTHIA | AUSTRIA

 ITALY

The Dolomites and the Rosengarten, the Sarentino Alps, and Pfunderer Mountains—Italy offers many special regions for hiking and climbing. Sometimes the fields are rugged, sometimes there are green meadow peaks—and everywhere huts that attract visitors with their hospitality and charm.

And even if every hut is as individual as the landscape and some are rustic, some chic and modern, many have a few things in common. On the one hand, there's history, which is not always glorious due to expropriation, mountain wars, and decay. On the other hand, there's the excellent cuisine; South Tyrolean specialties, for example. And ultimately it is the hosts who understand their profession and are there with warmth and openness to their guests and who make your stay unforgettable—just like the sublime landscape of the Italian Alps.

The Three Peaks are the symbol of the Dolomites and the Hochpustertal.

ITALY | TRENTO

The Holy One

The Lobbia Alta hut in the Adamello Group is a good base for high-altitude and ski tours–that's what Pope John Paul II also recognized.

RIFUGIO LOBBIA ALTA This hut enjoys a great location in the middle of the wide Adamello region. The Rifugio Lobbia Alta—also known as Rifugio Ai Caduti dell'Adamello—stands on the southern flank of the Lobbia Alta summit at almost 10,000 feet. Pope John Paul II visited the hut as part of a ski tour in 1984. He was at the hut again in 1988 and celebrated a mass at the Passo Lobbia Alta.

Not too long ago, hikers were happy about the good wood stove that kept the lounge of the Lobbia Alta hut warm because the windows were leaky, and it was particularly drafty in windy weather. At night, you needed a thick sleeping bag, and the water for washing your hands sometimes even froze in the barrel. It's no longer so cold in the hut today. Glacial decline was causing problems for the Lobbia Alta, which threatened to collapse in 2003. It then underwent an extensive renovation that cost several million euros; the hut didn't reopen until 2005. And thanks to the renovation, it is much more cozy and comfortable. The renovation also provided the hut with an independent power supply. Electricity is generated and stored with solar cells and vector hydrogen. The entire system is controlled by the university via remote maintenance.

The Adamello is the widest glacier area in the Eastern Alps. Anyone who has made their way from the Rifugio Lobbia Alta to Mount Ada-

ITALY | TRENTO | RIFUGIO LOBBIA ALTA

mello understands this. The terrain is almost flat over the mighty Adamello Glacier to the last summit ascent. When the sun is shining, this is a grandiose scene that almost reminds us of Arctic conditions. **When it's foggy, however, life quickly becomes uncomfortable and dangerous here, because it's very easy to lose your way.** The bell on the summit cross is intended to serve as an emergency signal in the event of fog.

In summer, glacial decline is increasingly obvious in the Adamello region. This brings to light many ugly artifacts of contemporary history. There is a lot of old ammunition and barbed wire in the region around the hut. Mountain war was waged here during the First World War; more people were killed by avalanches and the cold than by fighting. Hiking through these remnants makes clear the incredible suffering of that time. The construction of the Rifugio Lobbia Alta also dates back to the First World War. The first hut was built on the remains of former Italian barracks in 1920 at the south foot of Lobbia Alta

IN BRIEF

VALLEY TOWN Val di Genova

ALTITUDE 9,908 ft/3,020 m above sea level

OPEN mid-March to early May, mid-June to mid-September

ACCOMMODATIONS 100-bed dormitory, winter room with 8 beds

FOOD good Italian cuisine

GOOD TO KNOW The hut can only be reached via the glacier

RIFUGIO LOBBIA ALTA | TRENTO | ITALY 🇮🇹

Pope John Paul II used the granite altar with the big peace bell at the Passo della Lobbia Alta. He held a mass here in 1988, when he stopped at the hut for the second time in his life. (top)
Like a mirror, the mountain lake, which is surrounded by cotton grass, reflects the dreamlike backdrop of the Lobbia Alta. (below)

Climbing to the Rifugio Lobbia Alta requires crossing a glacier.

on the edge of the glacier. Not far from the hut, at the top of the Cresta della Croce, there is a large granite summit cross. It is dedicated in memory of the former Pope John Paul II. His visit left a lasting impression on the pious Italians. We understand only too well why he was so impressed by this lonely, wild mountain world. We are also captivated by the expanse of the glaciers, the hut's impressive location, and the panoramic view from the summit. And, of course, also by today's very cozy hut, which is run with great love and dedication by Romano and Martina, father and daughter. The food that is served in the wood-paneled parlor tastes excellent, and the hosts' friendly manner makes the stay even more pleasant. By the way, don't miss the night sky if it's clear, because the sky is a sea with countless stars—this breathtaking view is worth leaving a warm bed in the middle of the night! ❄

TOURS

TOUR 1 LOBBIA ALTA
Beautiful 10,000-foot peak, accessible from the hut with a bit of climbing. Magnificent panorama of the Adamello and Presanella
» 262 ft/80 m EG   » 1,574 ft/480 m
» 0.5 h   » medium

TOUR 2 RIFUGIO MANDRONE
Glaciers, granite slabs, sandy soil past Lago Nuovo and Lago Mandrone
» 1,969 ft/600 m EG   » 3.7 mi/6 km
» 2.5 h   » difficult

TOUR 3 CRESTA DELLA CROCE
Malga Bedole → Rifugio then climb to the ridge, then to the granite cross at the Cresta della Croce, then back to the hut
» 5,905 ft/1,800 m EG   » 5 mi/8.7 km
» 5.5 h   » difficult

ITALY | TRENTO | RIFUGIO LOBBIA ALTA

Lobbia Alta summer ski area

In a summer ski area, it's possible to ski even in the summer months—especially in June, July, and August. Due to the worldwide glacier decline since the 1990s, however, there are only very few of them left today.

The Lobbia Alta was one of the first summer ski resorts in Italy. In 1933, the Rifugio Lobbia Alta was expanded for the first time after its construction to provide enough space for the ski schools. Given its location in the middle of the Adamello Group, the hut was ideal as a base for skiing—at that time, the Mandrone Glacier was still right on the doorstep. Today, this is inconceivable, since the Rifugia is far above the glacier.

Although the Lobbia Alta is no longer a summer ski resort, in late winter the Lobbia Alta Hut is still considered an ideal starting or end point for ski tours.

Passionate skiers long for the ski resorts of past times, which could also be used in summer.

RIFUGIO LOBBIA ALTA | TRENTO | ITALY

237

ITALY | SOUTH TYROL

40

The 10,000-footers

DÜSSELDORFER HÜTTE (RIFUGIO SERRISTORI) The mountain village of Sulden is surrounded by many beautiful ten thousand-foot peaks. The Düsseldorfer Hütte is on the north side of the village high above the Zaytal. It not only offers a magnificent view of the Königspitze, Ortler, and Zebru, it is also a great base for several ten-thousand-foot peaks of varying difficulty.

We stand above the Düsseldorfer Hütte and pause for a moment. This view takes our breath away. Behind the hut on the other side of the valley, the Königspitze, Ortler, and Zebru rise up with their now largely snow-free north faces. The location that the Düsseldorf team chose for the construction of their hut in 1892 is great. The hut itself is run by the fifth generation of the Reinstadler family.

Many roads lead to Rome, it is said. In the same vein, one could say: Many trails lead to the Düsseldorfer Hütte! It is surrounded by several ten thousand-foot peaks of different difficulties. The Hohe Angelus and Vertainspitze are the main attractions. The quickest way to reach the Düsseldorfer hut is from the Kanzellift, which leads up from Sulden. A beautiful trail takes the hikers into the Zaytal and further up to the hut. If you arrive early, you can also climb the Hinteres Schöneck. Its summit is relatively easy to reach. There are only wire ropes over a few exposed rocks in the last few feet. The summit offers a great overview of the hiking area

Behind the Düsseldorfer Hütte there is a small mountain lake, which especially inspires the small hut guests.

ITALY | SOUTH TYROL | DÜSSELDORFER HÜTTE

around the Düsseldorfer Hütte. It is also possible to do this tour only on the last day and to descend from the summit to the north directly toward Sulden.

And in the midst of this wonderful landscape, where everyone will discover their own favorite trail, lies the Düsseldorfer Hütte. It is also an attractive destination for families with children, not least because of the small lake behind the hut. You can play and romp well here, and after a strenuous hike you can cool your feet in the clear water.

If your stomach is growling, you can look forward to a delicious meal from the hut's kitchen. Resi and her son Martin enjoy pampering their guests with South Tyrolean specialties. In addition to dumplings and noodles, Resi's legendary apple strudel is also on the menu. Don't miss it!

Happy and well-fed, you can rest in the evening—and enjoy the peace and quiet. In contrast to some other huts, where people share their sleeping quarters with lots of other people,

IN BRIEF

VALLEY TOWN Sulden

ALTITUDE 8,927 ft/2,721 m above sea level

OPEN mid-June to October

ACCOMMODATIONS 1 double room, 36 beds in multi-bed rooms, 15-bed dormitory, 6-bed winter room

FOOD nice warm South Tyrolean cuisine

GOOD TO KNOW You do not have to go back to the Kanzellift to descend from the hut. You can go straight down into the valley

DÜSSELDORFER HÜTTE | SOUTH TYROL | ITALY

The pink-blossoming cobweb houseleek often grows on rocks and rock rubble and in pastures and meadows. (top)
The rewarding but difficult Tschenglser Hochwand via ferrata leads over beautiful, airy rock passages to the summit. (below)

the rooms in the Düsseldorf hut are rather small. There are four-bed, five-bed, and six-bed rooms here, and the dormitories are also cozy, for they sleep a maximum of eight people. If you happen to share sleeping quarters with seven lumberjacks, that's just bad luck.

There's a toilet and washrooms on each floor. Warm water is available here, but there are no showers—something that doesn't bother most hikers, because they are used to this from other huts. In the end, the building's exposed location plays a role, for this often makes water supply difficult. And if you really want to refresh yourself, you can simply take a dip in the mountain lake behind the hut.

TOURS

TOUR 1 HINTERES SCHÖNECK
Relatively easy tour with view of the Ortler; hikers must not be afraid of heights
» 1,181 ft/360 m EG   » 1.9 mi/2 km
» 1.5 h   » medium

TOUR 2 TSCHENGLSER HOCHWAND VIA FERRATA
Challenging path to the summit through the southern falls of the Tschenglser Hochwand
» 2,132 ft/650 m EG   » 1 mi/3 km
» 3 h   » difficult

TOUR 3 HOHER ANGELUS
This ice-free tour ascends vertically via a via ferrata to the second-highest Laas peak
» 2,460 ft/750 EG   » 2 mi/3.3 km
» 3 h   » difficult

The Düsseldorfer Hütte as a panoramic window on the Ortler Alps.

241

ITALY | SOUTH TYROL | DÜSSELDORFER HÜTTE

Julius Payer

Across the way, on the Ortler, the Payerhütte is in an extremely exposed position on the Tabaretta Ridge at 9,937 feet. It is named after Julius Payer, who was not only an Austro-Hungarian officer, but also made a name for himself as a polar and alpine researcher, cartographer, and professor at the military academy, not to mention as a painter. One of his many achievements is the more than 60 first ascents in the Ortler Group. Among other things, he and his guide Johann Pinggera ascended the High Angelus and the Vertainspitze. He thus played a decisive role in making the summits around the Düsseldorfer Hütte accessible to us today.

Julius Payer was also active on the Ortler, the king of the South Tyrolean mountains, but not as a first ascender: He was the first to map the Ortler region. Today, the Payerhütte is a popular base for the Ortler ascent via the most frequently used normal route.

In the oil painting "Never Return," Julius Payer portrays himself and his team during the Austro-Hungarian North Pole Expedition of 1892.

242

DÜSSELDORFER HÜTTE | SOUTH TYROL | ITALY

HUT BOOK

HUT BOOK

The highest hut in the Alps: The Capanna Regina Margherita at an altitude of 14,940 feet

There are a few summit huts in the Alps, but none have such a great location as the Capanna Regina Margherita on the summit of the Signalkuppe in the Valais Alps. The construction of the hut began 1890; it was inaugurated in 1893 and dedicated to Queen Margarethe of Italy. She stayed overnight in the hut on August 18, 1893. The shelter was opened with a ceremony a little later in September. The current hut was built in 1980 and has a copper jacket that protects it from lightning.

Hikers ascend mainly from the south from Italy, in four hours from the Capanna Gnifetti. Due to the altitude, an overnight stay in the hut should not be underestimated. In the hut itself there is a scientific facility for high-altitude medical research.

It's clear that such a location often means that there is harsh weather—storms are a challenge against which the hut is also secured with ropes.

ITALY | SOUTH TYROL

41

The Treat

The Zufallhütte welcomes mountaineers to the breathtaking mountain world of the Ortler Group.

ZUFALLHÜTTE (RIFUGIO NINO CORSI)

The Zufallhütte in South Tyrol's Martello Valley is known for its good cuisine, whether you come for lunch during the day or stay overnight in the hut and enjoy the multi-course menu. The food in this hut is simply great. Hut host Ulli serves his tasty South Tyrolean cuisine with Italian influences.

The ascent is already a highlight, especially if you choose the Plima Gorge trail. It was built not long ago and has rightly developed directly into a popular excursion destination in the back of the Martello Valley. Some viewing platforms offer impressive deep views into the gorge of the Plima stream. Some of them hover vertically above the thunderous water. The absolute highlight, however, is the spectacular suspension bridge over the gorge.

But even the most beautiful trail will come to an end at some point, and you will be happy to put your tired feet up and recharge. And that's best done in the Zufallhütte. You will be warmly welcomed by the hut host, Ulli Müller. Old wooden ski poles and framed black-and-white photos that tell of times past hang on the hut's wooden walls. Fortunately, the original coziness is not a thing of the past, and so you can feel a very special charm in the Zufallhütte, something hikers appreciate.

The hut is particularly popular because of the good food. No matter what is put on the table here, it tastes delicious! And you may prefer

ITALY | SOUTH TYROL | ZUFALLHÜTTE

IN BRIEF

VALLEY TOWN Martell

ALTITUDE 7,431 ft/2,265 m above sea level

OPEN mid-February to early May and mid-June to mid-October

ACCOMMODATIONS 60 beds in double and multi-bed rooms, 20-bed dormitory

FOOD Excellent South Tyrolean cuisine with an Italian touch, extensive menu, friendly and fast service

GOOD TO KNOW There is a nice practice via ferrata behind the hut

Right near the Zufallhütte are beautiful mountain meadows (left), and also the small Heart of Jesus Chapel, built in 1915. (right)

to enjoy the Kaiserschmarrn (or goulash and dumplings or meat salad or spaghetti or whatever) on the terrace, because from here you have a wonderful mountain view. If the weather permits, you can also drink a beer and watch until the last ray of sunshine has disappeared behind the peaks, and enjoy the mood with new and old friends.

But then it's time to go to bed! Quiet hours in the Zufallhütte start at 10 p.m.—since many people want to be fit for their journeys the next day, but this is no problem. At 6 a.m. the next morning, the scent of freshly-brewed coffee wafts through the rustic hut and awakens the first guests.

There is a lot of hiking to be done around the hut. No matter if the Veneziaspitze, Köllkuppe, Butzenspitze, or Madritschspitze, all tours are wonderful, and each is special in its own way. These destinations are especially attractive in winter, when the deep snow glitters in the sun and dampens all the noise. Experienced ski mountaineers will also try their hand at Monte Cevedale or the Zufallspitze. If you

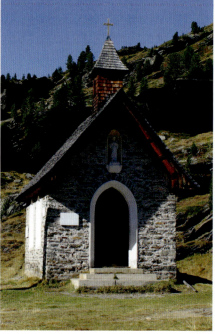

ZUFALLHÜTTE | SOUTH TYROL | ITALY

Culinary delights are very important at the Zufallhütte. The Kaiserschmarrn is simply wonderful.

return to the Zufallspitze after such a tour through ice and snow, you will enjoy the delicious dinner (today maybe taste the barley soup or perhaps the bacon platter with delicious smoked meats?) The sauna, which is located in a log cabin next to the hut and also helps cold toes warm up quickly, is especially popular. Instead of taking a shower afterwards, you can also jump right into the powder snow and boost your circulation.

Winter aside, the hut is also popular in the summer, when you can enjoy a great stay. The Madritschspitze now boasts a marked trail, something that did not appear on maps for a long time. There is probably no summit from which you can get a more beautiful view of the three peaks: Ortler, Königspitze, and Zebru.

TOURS

TOUR 1 PLIMA GORGE TRAIL
Adventurous trail from the Martell Valley to the Zufallhütte and back
» 984 ft/300 m EG   » 3 mi/6 km
» 2 h   » easy

TOUR 2 MURMELE VIA FERRATA
State-of-the-art via ferrata. Suitable for children
» 229 ft/70 m EG   » 426 ft/130 m
» 0.5 h   » medium

TOUR 3 MONTE CEVEDALE
Classic ski tour with flat climb across the Zufallferner; trail is more difficult near the summit and requires crampons
» 5,577 ft/1,700 m EG   » 11 mi/18 km
» 9 h   » difficult

ITALY | SOUTH TYROL | ZUFALLHÜTTE

A luxury hotel in the Martello Valley

If you take the Plima Gorge Trail to the Zufallhütte, you will pass a striking red building behind the reservoir at the end of the beautiful Martello Valley. This is the fascinating ruins of the former Hotel Paradiso, or the Hotel Albergo Sportivo Valmartello al Paradiso del Cevedale, as it was once called. It was built between 1933 and 1935 and was a luxury hotel with 250 beds and many amenities. For example, there was a post and telegraph office, a butcher, confectioner, hairdresser, masseur, ski instructors, reading room, and even a sauna. With the outbreak of the Second World War, it was confiscated by the Wehrmacht and used as a R&R facility for German soldiers. After the war, the hotel became more and more dilapidated. Today not much of the former splendor is left, but the ruins—enclosed by pine and larch trees and surrounded by ten thousand-foot peaks—have retained their air of mystery.

Although Hotel Paradiso's heyday did not last very long, the inhabitants of the Martello Valley never really cared for the building, which was so modern at the time. For the Martteller, it always remained a "garage."

ZUFALLHÜTTE | SOUTH TYROL | ITALY 🇮🇹

ITALY | SOUTH TYROL

In Snow and Ice

42

MÜLLERHÜTTE (RIFUGIO CIMA LIBERA)

The Müllerhütte is located on South Tyrolean soil directly above the mighty Übeltalferner on the south side of the Wilder Freiger. Its location directly above the glacier is ideal for ice training, crevasse salvage exercises, and even ice climbing events. In addition, the large peaks of the Stubai Alps are accessible from here.

Finally we are standing on the eastern ridge of the Wilder Freiger. It's not far to the summit of this high Stubai ten thousand-foot peak. But the final stretch is narrow and exposed. In addition, we are already tired, since we started from the Sulzenau hut very early this morning. The ascent to this point was long. We hiked past the beautiful Blaue Lacke and across the Fernerstube glacier to the Lübecker Trail. This old ascent was restored only a few years ago. We climbed up the secured ridge to this point. And now the question is how we will proceed. We decide to postpone the Wilder Freier until tomorrow and descend to the nearby Müllerhütte.

We are greeted in friendly fashion by the hut's host, Heidi. This Dane has been hosting the Müllerhütte for a few years. We enjoy the afternoon on the sunny terrace and find that we are inspired by the landscape. When the last ray of sunshine has finally disappeared behind the mountains, the cold drives even the bravest indoors. Then a cozy get-together and relaxed evening in the hut are on the program. Heidi

 The Ridnauntal is already behind the mountaineer— she still has to hike a bit to reach the Müllerhütte.

253

ITALY | SOUTH TYROL SOUTH TYROL | MÜLLERHÜTTE

IN BRIEF

VALLEY TOWNS Ridnaun-Maiern, Schönau Passeier

ALTITUDE 10,347 ft/3,154 m above sea level

OPEN early July to end of September

ACCOMMODATIONS 60 beds in shared rooms, 30-bed dormitory, no double rooms, heated 6-bed winter room

FOOD good South Tyrolean cuisine with friendly service

GOOD TO KNOW All ascents are long and demanding (glacier equipment required)

On the descent from the Wilder Freiger to the Müllerhütte, concentration is required. Many mountain accidents happen because of carelessness on the way back.

also likes to sit down with the hikers, for in the Müllerhütte, people appreciate telling stories and listening equally. And those who travel a lot in the mountains have certainly experienced a lot they can share with others.

The ingredients from which the simple, good meals are prepared at the Müllerhütte—the spaghetti that is obligatory in this region, and the dumplings and Kaiserschmarrn—have to be carried up the mountain, and in some cases supply flights also come by helicopter. This is not exactly a cakewalk, as anyone who makes their way to the Müllerhütte will notice. For to reach it, you inevitably have to cross a glacier. Of course, there are many glaciers in the Alps. But the fact that a hut can only be reached by crossing a glacier sets the Müllerhütte apart from most; there are only four other such huts throughout the Eastern Alps. The Rifugio Cima Libera, the Italian name of the Müllerhütte, is a true glacier hut! After the delicious food and the good mood in the lounge, most people still go to bed early, for those who still want to reach the Wilder Freiger need to start early the next

MÜLLERHÜTTE | SOUTH TYROL | ITALY

morning. You quickly reach the bottom of the glacier and cross the Übeltalferner toward the Becherhaus, which occupies a spectacular position on the summit of the Becher watching over the Übeltalferner. However, we leave it off to our right and reach the south ridge of the Freiger. With the help of the safety equipment, we turn across the block ridge up to the signal summit and over the narrow ridge to the summit cross. We are in the heart of the Stubai Alps, and the view of the surrounding mountain peaks is really magnificent. Of course, we are most pleased when the weather is good and there is bright sunshine. However, then it is also more difficult to say goodbye. And it's not only the mountain panorama to which you bid goodbye, but also the cozy hut on the glacier.

TOURS

TOUR 1 ZUCKERHÜTL
The highest Stubai peak. Attempt the classic Ostweg or the longer but easier Westweg
» 98 ft/750 HM   » 6.2 mi/4 km
» 3.5 h   » easy

TOUR 2 BECHERHAUS
Across the Übeltalferner, which crowns the peak of the Becher
» 220 ft/70 m EG   » 0.9 mi/1.5 km
» 0.75 h   » medium

TOUR 3 BOTZER
Remote summit across the Übeltalferner, return to the Müllerhütte. Best in early summer when snow conditions are good
» 1,574 ft/480 m EG   » 2.8 mi/4.5 km
» 3.5 h   » difficult

From the Müllerhütte, the trail leads over the Wilder Pfaff to the Zuckerhütl—the highest mountain in the Stubai Alps.

ITALY | SOUTH TYROL | MÜLLERHÜTTE

Ice Parade at the Müllerhütte

In snow and ice—the character of the Müllerhütte is also reflected in its events.

For many years, the so-called "Ice Parade" took place right near the hut; participants had to climb through a large crevasse. As many as 100, mostly young, climbers from South Tyrol, Austria, and Bavaria attended this event. You might think this would be highlight enough. But Heidi, the hospitable hut host, capped the event off each year by throwing a big party with live bands in her hut on the eve of the ice climbing competition. Each time there was dancing and partying until late into the night.

It requires a lot of physical conditioning, strength, and mountaineering experience to climb an overhanging ice wall.

MÜLLERHÜTTE | SOUTH TYROL | ITALY 🇮🇹

ITALY | SOUTH TYROL

43

The Changeling

FLAGGERSCHARTENHÜTTE (RIFUGIO FORCELLA VALLAGA) 56 years, a name change, and the eventful history of two world wars lay between the completion and the official inauguration of this idyllic hut in the Sarntal Mountains. To this day, it's actually a small miracle that people can rest and stay overnight here.

At first glance, the stone refuge on the small Flaggersee seems to melt into its surroundings. Located at the foot of the 8,992-foot Jakobsspitze, in the quiet seclusion of the Sarntal Valley, it hardly stands out during the day from the rocky landscape, which is covered by a green carpet of grasses and mosses in the summer months. In the evening, when the rocks reflect the warm red of the setting sun, the Flaggerschartenhütte also shines as if it were sending a grateful greeting to the universe every day.

This compact, two-story building has experienced so much in its more than 100-year existence. Built in 1910, the hut was marked by the eventful history of two world wars, even though it's difficult to imagine that war could ever reach this peacefully remote place. It all began as a transnational project between Germany and Austria, when the Alpine Club sections Marburg and Siegerland joined forces to build a shelter. The Marburg-Siegener-Hütte was to be inaugurated with ceremony in 1914. But World War I thwarted this plan. What followed were years of political uncertainty. A majority of the German and Austrian Alpine Club huts in South Tyrol were confiscated over the years.

In spring, when the cotton grass bears its fruit, the moor in front of the Flaggerschartenhütte is transformed into a sea of white cotton balls.

ITALY | SOUTH TYROL | FLAGGERSCHARTENHÜTTE

IN BRIEF

VALLEY TOWNS Durnholzer See/Durnholz, Losenheim, Puchberg, Mittewald

ALTITUDE 8,140 ft/2,481 m above sea level

OPEN end of May to mid-October

ACCOMMODATIONS 34-bed dormitory, 4 beds in the winter room

FOOD simple regional cuisine with local products Buffet breakfast from 7 a.m. to 8 a.m. Dinner at 6:30 p.m.

GOOD TO KNOW No dogs. Winter room has no stove

The Italian military occupied the current Flaggerschartenhütte, looted it, and let the building decay. But it was not forgotten. In the 1930s, the newly founded Brixen section of the Alpino Italiano tried to secure a lease and rescue the shelter from deterioration. But peace did not last long, because war overran the country again. Once again, there was an uninvited visit to the shores of the Flaggersee. And once again, the building fell into disrepair. After the end of the war, the Franzenfeste subsection took over the hut, renovated it, and officially opened it in 1960 under its current name.

But this wasn't easy. The long access roads to the hut and the lack of a material cableway made management as a hikers' hut a difficult undertaking from the very beginning. The hut's hosts, the Coccias, saved the Flaggerschartenhütte, since they approached the matter courageously and pragmatically. During their almost 25 years of hosting the hut, they made it an insider tip for hikers and ski tourers who were looking for peace and authenticity off the beaten tourist paths.

FLAGGERSCHARTENHÜTTE | SOUTH TYROL | ITALY

The ups and downs of a mountain hut depend not least on the host. Since 2019, the hospitality team of Maura and Mauro has been hosting the Flaggerschartenhütte. Under their recent leadership, things are going well again in this lonely high valley. The historic hut is considered a popular stop and offers beds for 34 guests. Even in winter, ski touring enthusiasts can take shelter here, but there's only space for four people. Mauro rules the kitchen. It's important to him that ingredients be local, and it's clear to diners that all dishes are homemade. In the morning there is a breakfast buffet - a special feature that you won't find in every mountain hut.

TOURS

TOUR 1 TAGEWALDHORN
Marked trail leads N; short, ascent with wire ropes across a rock face. Ascend to the summit via the steep east ridge
» 689 ft/210 m EG   » 1.2 mi/2 km
» 1.5 h   » medium

TOUR 2 JAKOBSSPITZE
The hut's local mountain is to the S via a marked trail that leads across scree
» 788 ft/240 m EG   » 0.75 mi/1.2 km
» 1 h   » easy

TOUR 3 HORSESHOE TOUR
7-day hike in the Sarntal Alps; a must for ambitious mountaineers: earn the "Golden Horseshoe"
» 19,750 ft/6,020 m EG   » 58 mi/94 km
» 33 h   » difficult

There is no time of day when the Dolomites are as beautiful to look at as in the morning—which, as we know, is the golden hour.

ITALY | SOUTH TYROL | FLAGGERSCHARTENHÜTTE

Rambazamba

Many hut hosts have already learned that the wind can roar over the Flaggerschartenhütte at a very rapid pace. Among them the Niederkofler family, who found part of the hut roof in the Flaggersee after a particularly violent storm.

Vibrations of a different kind lay in the air when Elisabeth Illmer hosted the hut. For many years, visitors found peace and meditative relaxation here, not least thanks to a wide range of courses and events. As a passionate yodeler, Elisabeth herself regularly made joyful noise and taught interested people this art. Whether with or without a training session: Hearty yodeling is absolutely recommended.

A storm in the mountains is impressive: Rain streams down, gusts of wind sweep over the mountain peaks, thunder roars through the valleys—behind the protective wall of a mountain hut, all this is no problem.

FLAGGERSCHARTENHÜTTE | SOUTH TYROL | ITALY

HUT BOOK

264

HUT BOOK

Old (bivouac) boxes: Sometimes charming, sometimes horrible: Emergency camps of a special kind

Thus far in this book, we have only presented hosted huts. But there are bivouac boxes for special activities and emergencies. Sometimes these are in good condition, sometimes they are quite neglected. While they are more of an emergency shelter in Germany, Austria, Switzerland, Slovenia, and France, a veritable bivouac culture prevails, especially in Italy. The boxes are gladly included in tour planning here.

Which bivouac boxes are our highlights? We like the Rhineland-Palatinate bivouac on the Mainzer Höhenweg. The Günther-Messner bivouac on the Hochferner is an important base for the Hochfeiler Nordwand, and the Lalidererspitze bivouac is in the middle of a lunar landscape in the Karwendel Mountains. The wide selection allows everyone to find their own favorite.

Like a snail from its (oversized) house, this bright red bivouac box in Lombardy peeks out from underneath a mighty boulder.

ITALY | SOUTH TYROL

The Historic One

SCHLERNHAUS (RIFUGIO BOLZANO) For 140 years, the Rifugio Bolzano, as the Schlernhaus is called in Italian, has stood on the high plateau of the mighty Sciliar, not far from the mountain's highest point. It has survived wind and weather, not to mention two devastating world wars. The house itself is always the subject of political discussion, as it is of great importance to both the German and Italian language groups.

We already have a long day behind us when the thunderstorms start. Although we are already on the wide plateau of the Sciliar and it's not far to the hut, we're too far away to arrive there with dry feet. The thunderstorm strikes us so suddenly that we don't even have time to put on our rain gear. When we finally reach the hut, we are dripping wet. Well, that's certainly a welcome!

As compensation for the wet start, the Schlernhaus presents its best face. Silvia and Harald take care of "their" hut and guests with a lot of passion; after all, the Schlernhaus has been family-owned since the 1970s and they took it over from their parents in 1999. They work hard to put tasty and invigorating South Tyrolean dishes on the table. In addition to the meal—don't forget to try the barley soup—there's the view of the mountain panorama through the dining room's large windows. Meanwhile, our wet clothes are drying. Thanks to the fireplace, you

In the evening, the sunset bathes the Rosengarten—the mountain massif behind the Schlernhaus—in soft yellows.

267

ITALY | SOUTH TYROL | SCHLERNHAUS

IN BRIEF

VALLEY TOWN Fiè allo Sciliar

ALTITUDE 8,061 ft/2,457 m above sea level

OPEN June to September

ACCOMMODATIONS 15 double rooms, 40 beds in multi-bed rooms, 57-bed dormitory, heated winter room

FOOD high-quality, regional dishes with typical South Tyrolean dishes

GOOD TO KNOW When climbing over Fiè, luggage can be transported to the hut by prior arrangement. Washrooms with two hot-water showers

The mixture of trails through lush green meadows up to the stony Rosszahnscharte makes the tour through the Rosengarten Nature Park an experience.

can also warm up in the dining room, so you can enjoy other people's company after the meal.

Then you can enjoy one of the 120 beds that await exhausted hikers. You have the choice between a bed in a double or single room, or you can choose a bed in the dormitory. Blankets are available, but especially in autumn and spring you should bring a sleeping bag, because it can get cold in the bedrooms. Hut sleeping bags are also mandatory in summer for hygienic reasons. But an experienced hut hiker already knows that. After all, this is one of the three items that you should have in every mountain hut: Slippers, a towel, and a hut sleeping bag.

If the kids get bored or the weather is too bad to be outside, the Schlernhaus also has a few board games to pass time in the hut.

And by the way: The history of the Schlernhaus is remarkable. After the First World War, it was confiscated from the German-speaking Alpine Club of Bolzano and transferred to the Italian Club Alpino Italiano. Attempts to transfer the hut back to the South Tyrol Alpine Club after the Second World War failed. Even today,

SCHLERNHAUS | SOUTH TYROL | ITALY

the ownership of the Schlernhaus is still a topic of discussion among long-established members of the Alpine Club Bolzano and the Club Alpino Italiano.

The next day, you have to get up early to climb the Petz, the highest point on the Sciliar. A little later, when the sun rises, all troubles will be forgotten. What a wonderful miracle! The Rosengarten massif begins to glow in the rays of the morning sun. This was predicted in the legend of King Laurin: Laurin once cursed the Rosengarten. It should not be visible during the day or at night. But Laurin had forgotten the twilight, and so it happens that the enchanted garden still makes its "stone roses" shine for a short time. The red glow of the rocks at dusk is today known as Enrosadira (alpine glow).

TOURS

TOUR 1 ALPE DI SIUSI THE
Long but easy circular trail through the Schlern-Rosengarten Nature Park. Tierser-Alpl-Hütte, (below the jagged rocky peaks of the Rosszähne) → Mahlknechthütte, → Alpe di Siusi. Return to the Schlernhaus via the Saltnerhütte
» 98 ft/1,150 HM   » 6.2 mi/23 km
» 7.5 h   » easy

TOUR 2 TSCHAFONHÜTTE
Schlernhaus → Moarboden and Sesselschwaige, then rest. Climb to the Tschafonhütte via the Prügelsteig in the Schlernbachtal and forest path in the Mangaduierbachtal. Alternative route: Nigglberg via ferrata
» 984 ft/300 m EG   » 5.0 mi/8 km
» 3.5 h   » difficult

Against the wonderful backdrop of the Rosengarten, Haflinger horses enjoy the lush green pasture.

269

ITALY | SOUTH TYROL | SCHLERNHAUS

The Mountain of Legends

There are many legends, not just about the Rosengarten, but also the Sciliar. Many of these are about the Sciliar witches, often in connection with severe storms that they are said to have caused around the Sciliar. If you want to believe the legends, a dwarf is said to have eavesdropped on the witches when they made a plan. The plan provided for a devastating storm that would completely destroy the entire area. The dwarf also heard that this plan could only be thwarted by ringing a church bell. Of course, the dwarf immediately informed the first priest he could find, and was thus able to mitigate the storm and save the area.

Today, the motif of witches is used in the surrounding villages in the form of dolls and statues. On the Puflatsch at the Alpe di Siusi there are striking stone formations, called witch benches, on which the witches, according to legend, still like to settle today and enjoy the spectacular view. And regardless of whether you believe in the old tales or not—you should definitely do as the legends say and have a seat.

Are the Sciliar witches behind the impending storm? It's certain that the clouds around the legendary Sciliar give it a mystical aura.

SCHLERNHAUS | SOUTH TYROL | ITALY

ITALY | SOUTH TYROL

45

A Climber's Paradise

At the foot of the Vajolettürme, the Rifugio Re Alberto has established its location in the "Gartl"-Schuttkar—an ideal starting point for climbing tours.

GARTLHÜTTE (RIFUGIO RE ALBERTO I)

The Rifugio Re Alberto, which has found its place in the heart of the Rosengarten massif, owes its German name to its location in a "Gartl" called Schuttkar. It is surrounded by the huge mountain fortresses of the Dolomites, such as the Laurinswand, the Kesselkogel Nordwand, and the famous Vajolettürme, Delago, Stabeler, and Winklerturm, on which climbing history has been written. Today, they are certainly some of the most impressive rock towers in the Alps and are still very popular climbing destinations.

We are standing at the door of the Gartlhütte, and we are happy to have arrived at last. We haven't seen how beautiful the hut's location is yet. Today was simply too long. After an early start, we arrived at the Karerpass and took the chairlift to the Kölner Hütte. Then we tackled the via ferrata to the Santner Pass—a true classic in the Dolomites that should not be underestimated. The secured areas start quite high up; before that, we have to climb some unsecured rocks, Which sets our adrenaline racing. When we get out of the via ferrata at the Santner Pass, our nerves relax and first we sit in the sun. Now the leisurely descent to today's destination, the Gartlhütte, awaits.

ITALY | SOUTH TYROL | GARTLHÜTTE

IN BRIEF

VALLEY TOWNS Gardeccia (Trento), Welschnofen (South Tyrol)

ALTITUDE 8,599 ft/2,621 m above sea level

OPEN mid-June to end of September

ACCOMMODATIONS 60-room dormitory, 4-bed winter room

FOOD A successful mixture of Tyrolean and Italian cuisine

GOOD TO KNOW The Santnerpass via ferrata is very impressive

On the via ferrata to the Paternkofel, hikers enjoy a fantastic view of Lago dei Piani, the Schusterplatte, and the Altensteinspitz.

Once you arrive, you should not be in too much of a hurry to make camp, because the hut's ambiance is just great; take some time to enjoy it properly. The three Vajolettürme are so close you could almost touch them. They point right up toward the sky.

The first Gartlhütte was built in 1929. The famous mountaineer Tita Piaz bought the hut in 1933 and opened the Rifugio Re Alberto in I., which was named in honor of the Belgian king Albert I, with whom Piaz traveled some routes in the Dolomites.

Piaz was a gifted climber and was also called the "Devil of the Dolomites" due to his incomprehensible skills . He developed the Piaz climbing technique that is named after him. However, he came too late for the first ascent of the Vajolettürmen. Nevertheless, he left his mark on the towers in the following years. He developed many routes there. He also opened the most popular climbing route on the southwest edge of the Delagoturm—also known as the Delagokante—in 1911. His hut provided

GARTLHÜTTE | SOUTH TYROL | ITALY

ideal base in the middle of a climber's paradise. Another monument is the Piazturm, which he first climbed in 1899; it is named for him.

Meanwhile, we enjoy the delicious cuisine in the hut, which features both Tyrolean and Italian specialties. The hut itself has acquired the charm of a real mountain accommodation in recent years. There are cozy rooms with three and four beds as well as a large dormitory room. In the evening, we treat ourselves to a glass of red wine in the dining room in addition to the delicacies provided by the kitchen—this is almost a must at an Italian hut.

The next morning, we descend toward the Vajolethütte. The climb winds impressively down through the steep gorge. We enjoy magnificent views and review our trip. All of us agree: Both the Santner Pass and the overnight stay at the Gartlhütte will remain etched in our memory.

TOURS

TOUR 1 SANTNER PASS ASCENT
Via ferrata requires courage. Can be combined with the Rotwand or the Masare via ferrata
» 3,149 ft/960 m EG   » 4.7 mi/7.5 km
» 5 h   » medium

TOUR 2 KESSELKOGEL
Across the Grasleitenhang to the Kesselkogel summit. Final stage is a short ladder
» 2,395 ft/730 m EG   » 6.2 mi/5 km
» 3.5 h   » medium

TOUR 3 STABELERTURM
"Fehrmann" plaisir tour to middle summit of the Vajolettürme in 6 IV-degree pitches
» 656 ft/200 m EG   » 0.4 mi/0.6 km
» 5 h   » difficult

The Vajolettürme are not only popular with climbers: There's a high line at a dizzying height between the Delagoturm and the Stabelerturm.

275

ITALY | SOUTH TYROL | GARTLHÜTTE

King Laurin's garden

Even if we have already briefly touched on the legend about the dwarf king Laurin on the Sciliar, we have to mention it again here. Because here in the Gartl, where the Rifugio Re Alberto stands, according to the popular alpine legend, is where King Laurin's beautiful rose garden was. One day, Laurin kidnapped the prince of Bolzano's daughter, with whom he had fallen in love. The knight Dietrich of Bern then set out to retrieve the prince's daughter. He met the dwarf king, who was armed with a magic belt and his camouflage cap, which made him invisible, in the Rosengarten. Nevertheless, Dietrich was able to defeat the king by beating him to the place where the roses moved—and Laurin was hiding. The roses had betrayed the king. In anger, Laurin cursed his beloved roses, which immediately turned to stone so that no one could see them anymore. It's only in the glow at sunrise and sunset that they are still visible today.

→

At dusk, it's possible to think that you're looking at the dwarf king Laurin's red rose garden.

GARTLHÜTTE | SOUTH TYROL | ITALY

ITALY | SOUTH TYROL

46

The Handy One

TIERSER ALPL HÜTTE (RIFUGIO ALPE DI TIRES) Between the Rosengarten and the Sciliar is the Tierser Alpl Hütte—a very comfortable and modern shelter. It's hard to believe that the first shelter here was created entirely by hand. Max Aichner began building the hut by himself in 1957. Since then, it has been extended several times, making it more and more comfortable.

Thunderstorms are rolling across the Sciliar and the Rosengarten. We made it to the hut just in time to stay dry. It's the first day of our planned Rosengarten crossing. Our route took us from the Kompatsch cable car station on the Alpe di Siusi via the Mahlknechthütte and the Dialer Kirchl to the Tierser Alpl Hütte. Shortly before reaching our destination, we still had time to observe the marmots playing along the trail. We deliberately chose not to take the more impressive route over the Rosszahnscharte. This seemed too dangerous to us due to the unpredictable weather conditions.

The hut's comforts surprise us. The rooms sleep a maximum of eight people, there are clean washrooms, showers, and a shoe drying room. Everything is made of light wood and looks very friendly, almost like a piece of Scandinavia in the middle of the Alps. The hut was being rebuilt when we were here a few years ago. However, the Aichner family extended a friendly greeting nevertheless.

The food is also excellent. The hosts Stefan and Judith love good food and they spoil their

← The modern Tierser Alpl Hütte, which was awarded the South Tyrolean Architecture Prize, stands at the foot of the bizarre Rosszähne formation in the Dolomites.

279

ITALY | SOUTH TYROL | TIERSER ALPL HÜTTE

IN BRIEF

VALLEY TOWN Fiè allo Sciliar

ALTITUDE 8,018 ft/2,444 m above sea level

OPEN end of May to mid-October

ACCOMMODATIONS 5 double rooms, 64 beds in multi-bed rooms, 53-bed dormitory, 6-bed winter room

FOOD good Tyrolean cuisine with a Mediterranean touch, regional ingredients

GOOD TO KNOW In stable weather, make sure to take the route across the Rosszahnscharte

guests accordingly. They serve Tyrolean cuisine with a Mediterranean touch. The ingredients come almost entirely from the region. For example, the menu includes boiled beef with roasted potatoes or the house specialty, the Tierser-Alpl plate with polenta and tomatoes, topped with cheese and baked. And because you can treat yourself to something sweet after a hike, there are various strudels and cakes for dessert.

These two hosts have been managing the hut for about 30 years. Judith took over the hut from her father Max. After the Second World War, he felt he had few choices in life. Emigrating from his beloved mountains was no alternative for him, so he bought a 2152-square-foot plot of land under the Rosszähnen. In 1957, he set off alone with a wheelbarrow and a pickaxe to build a hut up there. It took him six years to complete it.

He also built the Maximilian via ferrata over the Rosszähne and the Laurenzi via ferrata, which he named after his wife Laura. The latter is on our agenda for the next day. It's an exciting

Blueberries (above) and lingonberries (below) are also at home in the Alps, to the delight of many hikers.

280

TIERSER ALPL HÜTTE | SOUTH TYROL | ITALY

TOURS

TOUR 1 MAXIMILIAN VIA FERRATA
Highest point of the Sciliar plateau; the Roterdspitze involves the ascent to the Grosser Rosszahn and over the Roterdscharte
» 787 ft/240 m EG   » 3.1 mi/5 km
» 3.5 h   » easy

TOUR 2 PLATTKOFELHÜTTE
Trail no. 4 through alpine meadows to the Plattkofelhütte. If you wish, you can still climb the Sassolungo
» 590 ft/180 m EG   » 4 mi/6.5 km
» 2 h   » medium

TOUR 3 GRASLEITEN CIRCUIT
Tierser Alpl → Molignon Pass → Grasleitenhütte; return through the Bärenloch
» 2,625 ft/800 m EG   » 5 mi/8 km
» 5 h   » medium

rock adventure that requires safe weather conditions. Today we are lucky, because the thunderstorms have dissipated and the sun is smiling at us in the morning. We climb from the hut up to the Molignon Pass. The view becomes more spectacular with every foot of elevation. The hut's red roof shines in the sun, and the Rosszähne rise above it. The via ferrata, unlike many other routes in the Rosengarten, is relatively quiet, because it is a bit off the main routes, but its difficulties should not be underestimated. Overall, we enjoy a great hike over an exposed ridge in the eastern Rosengarten, one that started with a relaxing night in the Tierser Alpl Hütte. We think of Max Aichner and his pioneering spirit between the Sciliar and Rosengarten.

Between the Sciliar, Sassolungo, and the Rosengarten south of the Alpe di Siusi, the Tierser Alpl Hütte sits in the Tierser Sattel.

🇮🇹 ITALY | SOUTH TYROL

47

The Green One

BRIXNER HÜTTE (RIFUGIO BRESSANONE)

Surrounded by a wreath of green mountain peaks, the Brixner Hütte is located on the edge of the Pfannealm, a magnificent plateau in the Pfunderer Mountains characterized by pastures and steep hillsides. Because it is located on the Pfunderer Höhenweg, long-distance hikers like to use this hut as a base.

Cell phone reception? Nope! That's all the better, because then you can simply sit back, and since nobody can call you, nothing disturbs the peace. There's also no need to talk a lot, because the panorama, which is best viewed from the terrace of the Brixner Hütte, is so impressive that it takes your breath away. The mountain slopes are green right up to the top. This does hikers good, for often they only have bare gray rock or ice to look at once they reach their high-altitude destinations. Of course, this view reminds many people of the Allgäu, even if this region is less well-known. The Brixner Hütte is a place to which people like to return.

On the one hand, that's due to the beautiful hikes that you can take from here. You can explore the two ten thousand-foot peaks, the Wilde Kreuzspitze and the Wurmaulspitze, or there's the Pfannspitze. On the other hand, this is due to the hut's charm. It's quite small and therefore very comfortable. There is good South Tyrolean cuisine, and the hut team that supports Simon, Christoph, and Magda takes loving care of their guests. As part of the German Alpine Club's "This is how the mountains taste"

← Embedded in the lush green mountain landscape, it's possible think that the Brixner Hütte is in New Zealand. But far from it—such enchanting nature can also be found in the South Tyrol.

283

ITALY | SOUTH TYROL | BRIXNER HÜTTE

IN BRIEF

VALLEY TOWN Vals

ALTITUDE 7,486 ft/2,282 m above sea level

OPEN early June to mid-October

ACCOMMODATIONS 37-bed dormitory, 6-bed winter room

FOOD high-quality, traditional dishes

GOOD TO KNOW Ascent to the Fanealm is only permitted between 9 a.m. and 5 p.m. in summer. Otherwise, a bus leaves from Vals

If you're lucky, you will encounter marmots on the way to the Brixner Hütte.

campaign, the Brixner Hütte prepares delicious food from regional ingredients. Especially delicious are the shepherd's macaroni (Italian maccheroni alla pastora) and the barley soup, but the buckwheat dumplings with cheese are a dream that one does not often dare to dream in mountain huts. There is delicious apricot cake or strudel for dessert.

The hut offers beds for 40 in its dormitory. That's why in the evening, when the day hikers are on their way home, it is much quieter and more comfortable. You can enjoy the last rays of sunshine over the green peaks or gather around the table to play cards in rainy weather.

A hut was opened in this fascinating location for the first time in 1909; at that time, it was a self-catering hut. However, this hut's fate was the fate of many South Tyrolean huts. It was confiscated during the First World War and it fell into disrepair after the Second World War. It was not until the 1970s that a new hut was built. 20 years later it was expanded again and since that time, it has been inviting hikers to

BRIXNER HÜTTE | SOUTH TYROL | ITALY

enjoy its idyll and its hospitality. A mandatory tour before leaving these green mountains takes hikers to the Wurmaulspitze. It is the hut's mountain, and at just over 10,000 feet, it's a really beautiful summit destination. The trail climbs steeply and across the green slopes. Honestly, the tour is not that difficult. Only in the last section does a rock step get in hikers' way. You have to be careful here and climb carefully over to the summit cross. The summit offers the opportunity to say goodbye to this special area. For it's not always the highest peaks that people remember, but sometimes the quiet and tranquil mountains, such as the Wurmaulspitze and the Wilde Kreuzspitze.

TOURS

TOUR 1 WILDER SEE
Trail between the peaks of the Wilder Kreuzspitze and the Rauhtaljoch
» 1,738 ft/530 m EG   » 3.1 mi/5 km
» 2.5 h   » easy

TOUR 2 WILDE KREUZSPITZE
Ascent to the summit of the Pfunderer Mountains; suitable for physically fit hikers
» 2,559 ft/780 m EG   » 2.2 mi/3.6 km
» 2.5 h   » medium

TOUR 3 PFUNDERER HÖHENWEG
Multi-day tour S of the Alpenhauptkamm through the Pfunderer Mountains: Sterzing → St. Georgen/Brunico
» 18,307 ft/5,580 m EG   » 45 mi/72 km
» 30 h   » difficult

Steep serpentines bring ambitious hikers to the Wurmaulspitze. Their efforts are rewarded by the fabulous view of the Wilde Kreuzspitz and the Valsertal.

285

ITALY | SOUTH TYROL | BRIXNER HÜTTE

The alpine village of Fane

Created in the Middle Ages as a hospital for plague and cholera victims, this rustic alpine village in the Valsertal has one of the most beautiful alpine pastures in South Tyrol. The village consists of about 30 buildings and it is surrounded by a unique mountain and natural backdrop. There are houses and hay barns, plus a small church. The houses' rustic character captivates visitors. During the summer, farmers live here to cultivate the alpine pasture. In some huts, it is also possible to stop at any time of year and taste a fresh glass of milk from cows in the alpine pasture. This makes Fane the ideal place to get in the mood for the hike to the Brixner Hütte.

Embedded in a unique mountain and natural landscape, there are a total of 30 buildings, houses and hay barns, a small church, and three alpine pubs, scattered across the mountain village of Fane.

BRIXNER HÜTTE | SOUTH TYROL | ITALY 🇮🇹

ITALY | SOUTH TYROL

48

The Wild One

PISCIADÙ HÜTTE (RIFUGIO FRANCO CAVAZZA AL PISCIADÙ) Sparse, rugged, jagged—the mighty Sella massif of the Dolomites. A world almost like another planet. In the middle of this rocky wilderness, the Pisciadù Hütte watches over the Grödnerjoch Pass road. Deep blue Lake Pisciadù makes the landscape even more perfect.

Surrounded by bizarre rock formations at the Pisciadù Hut, hikers might ask themselves whether they're still on earth at all.

We're in front of the crowning conclusion of the Pisciadù via ferrata: The famous suspension bridge. It's not difficult to cross it; after all, the bridge was built of solid wood. But the scenery in this wildly rugged Dolomite landscape is really very impressive.

The Pisciadù via ferrata is the absolute hit in the truest sense of the word—hikers flock from near and far to this justifiably famous via ferrata. A short approach, spectacular landscapes, a medium difficulty level, and a great hut are the reasons for a beautiful via ferrata day. The Pisciadù Trail is very special; it includes crossing a waterfall, climbing a vertical row of grips, and the steep climb on the impressive Exnerturm. However, you will have to share this experience with many like-minded people, especially on weekends. We happened on a relatively quiet day in autumn.

After the bridge, it's an easy hike. A little later, we're sitting on the terrace of the Pisciadù Hütte, enjoying the view and the delicious Ladin cuisine, which promises hearty dumplings and a delicious apple strudel as dessert. We can thus recharge the strength we have used up on the

ITALY | SOUTH TYROL | PISCIADÙ HÜTTE

IN BRIEF

VALLEY TOWNS Alta Badia, Colfosco

ALTITUDE 8,487 ft/2,587 m above sea level

OPEN early June to end of September

ACCOMMODATIONS 76 beds, 100-bed dormitory

FOOD good South Tyrolean and Ladin cuisine

GOOD TO KNOW A helmet is a must here

Not much can happen on the well-secured wooden suspension bridge of the Pisciadù via ferrata. Nevertheless, some people feel sick to their stomachs when crossing.

next day. The view from the terrace is impressive. The view sweeps from the turquoise Lake Pisciadù to the peaks of the Cima Pisciadù, the Sassongher, the Cir, and over to the Fanes Group. The happiest are those hikers who visit the hut in good weather, because the blazing alpine glow is something you won't forget so quickly if you see it up here. And then there's the starry sky! Some people would probably prefer to spend the night outdoors under this blanket of countless sparkling stars rather than under the woolen blankets on the bunk beds inside the hut—even though they are so cozy. The Bamberg section built the first hut on this site in 1902. For a long time, its fate was uncertain. After the First World War, it was confiscated and mostly ignored.

It was not until the takeover by Club Alpino Italiano after the Second World War that the hut was expanded.

PISCIADÙ HÜTTE | SOUTH TYROL | ITALY

A worthwhile destination is the Cima Pisciadù, which is located only about 1,312 feet elevation gain from the hut.

Today, via ferrata climbers are the most frequent guests, but hikers also find their way to the hut via the Val Setus. This is partially exposed, secured with wire ropes, and requires great concentration in some places. The path through the impressive Val Mezdi is the best choice for the descent. If you want to go even higher, you can take on the Cima Pisciadù, which you can reach through the Val de Tita and over the Bamberger Sattel. You will finally reach the summit cross after hiking across scree and simple rocks.

TOURS

TOUR 1 PIZ BOÈ
Steep uphill trail to wide high plateau and through the rugged Sella to the Boe Hütte. Boe summit is a worthwhile detour
»2,132 feet/650 m EG »2.8 mi/4.5 km
»3 h » medium

TOUR 2 VAL GARDENA CIRCUIT
Scenic multi-day tour above Val Gardena; starts and ends at cable car valley station in Urtijei. You pass a total of 9 huts
»15,092 feet/4,600 m EG »38.5 mi/62 km
»25 h » medium

🇮🇹 ITALY | SOUTH TYROL | PISCIADÙ HÜTTE

Ladin

Ladin food is served at the Pisciadù Hütte. But what is Ladin actually? On the one hand, it's the third language in the Dolomites, in addition to Italian and German. The Ladin language developed from a mixture of the Celtic and Rhaetian languages with Latin. It was once the most widely spoken language in the Alps. After the barbarian migration, however, it gradually withdrew in favor of Italian and could only hold on in some protected valleys. Today, it is recognized as the third national language in South Tyrol. On the other hand, Ladin generally refers to a type of culture. Ladin culture is still very anchored in the Val Badia. That's why the food served in the Pisciadù Hütte contains elements of Ladin cuisine. The latter has its roots in traditional farmer's recipes, for farmers were able to conjure up tasty dishes from a few ingredients—for example, "turtes," fried dumplings filled with spinach or sauerkraut.

The Ladin cuisine, which is strongly associated with the Alta Badia region, consists of simple, down-to-earth dishes.

PISCIADÙ HÜTTE | SOUTH TYROL | ITALY 🇮🇹

HUT BOOK

Hut fauna: "Wild West" behind the hut

Huts are especially frequented destinations in summer. Wild animals only linger here if they have grown very used to people. Then they almost come to the hut. Particularly worth mentioning are the ibex around the Rüsselsheimer Hütte in the Pitztal. But people also see marmots time and time again. We watched them play at the Tierser Alpl Hütte once. Other animals that you see again and again at huts are chamois. But it's not just the wild animals that excite us. Many huts also have their own animals, which especially delight children. Whether llamas, donkeys, pigs, rabbits, or goats. These lovable creatures make people happy. This results in exciting offerings such as a llama trek to the Medelser Hütte.

People are briefly perplexed when asked whether these striking peaks are really the Drei Zinnen, because llamas are not usually found in the Dolomites.

ITALY | VENETO

The Oldest One in the Dolomites

The striking boulders of the Dolomites rise out of the earth like a miracle of nature. All this can be viewed admirably from the terrace of the Nuvolau Hütte.

RIFUGIO NUVOLAU The Rifugio Nuvolau has crowned a narrow cliff in the Ampezzo Dolomites for nearly 140 years. The shelter is still small and authentic, almost as if time had stopped for years on end. The location, with a fantastic view of Monte Antelao, Monte Pelmo, and Civetta, is especially majestic.

We got up early this morning. The alarm clock rang long before breakfast, which starts at 7:00 a.m. In the past, we have heard a lot about the spectacular sunrise on the Nuvolau, how it is bathed in red. Today we are seeing it for the first time with our own eyes. Slowly, the sun rises over the Sorapis massif, and the early morning and the valley basin of Cortina d'Ampezzo are bathed in a beautiful light. Leaving a warm bed early was more than worthwhile. In the mountains, it's often these small moments of harmony with nature and the grandeur of the landscape that people remember.

Afterwards we refresh ourselves at breakfast in the hut, to be fit for our day's agenda. Yesterday we hiked over from the Falzarego Pass. An easy trail took us to the Averauscharte. Again and again we had to turn around and admire the impressive Hexenstein, the massive Lagazuoi, and the mighty Tofana di Rozes. At the gorge you can see the Dolomite Queen, the Marmolada, and the Piz Boè. Now we cross under the mighty south face of the Averau to the Averauhütte. The Averau rocks are still in our shoes on its via ferrata and then we climb over easy rock steps up to

ITALY | VENETO | RIFUGIO NUVOLAU

IN BRIEF

VALLEY TOWN Cortina d'Ampezzo

ALTITUDE 8,444 ft/2,574 m above sea level

OPEN mid-June to mid-September

ACCOMMODATIONS 16 beds in 4 multi-bed rooms, 8-bed dormitory

FOOD simple, traditional, authentic, good Italian cuisine

GOOD TO KNOW Short, easy access to the hut from the chairlift. Authentic hut equipped with the essentials

Nuvolau with its summit hut. Opened with ceremony on August 11, 1883, it is the oldest hut in the Dolomites. Its construction dates back to the Saxon Colonel Richard von Meerheimb, who was cured of a severe lung disease in Cortina d'Ampezzo and made a contribution to the local Alpine Association for the construction of a hut for this reason. The builders chose the beautiful spot on the Nuvolau. As a thank you to the donor, the hut was also called the Sachsendankhütte in the beginning. Today it belongs to the Cortina section of the Club Alpino Italiano, and it has been hosted by the Siorpaes family for over 30 years. Here people follow old customs, so the experience at the hut remains authentic and original.

Since there is no water on top of the mountain, water must be transported by suspension train from the Cinque Torri Hütte. That's why you can't expect a shower up here in this small hut. You should instead enjoy its authenticity and the beautiful sunrises. The hut's food is also a point in favor of the Rifugio Nuvolau. In the

RIFUGIO NUVOLAU | VENETO | ITALY

midst of all the simplicity and traditional flair, the Sachertorte is an unexpected treat. You should definitely reserve a bed in advance, as the rooms—all equipped with a premium view of Cortina, the Giau Pass, and the Marmolata—get booked out fast.

After we've had our breakfast, we head to the Ra Gusela via ferrata. Immediately after the hut, the first shaky ladder is waiting for us. After a beautiful plateau come the next steep section, which we climb with appropriate caution. Finally, a long trail leads to the mountain station of the Cinque Torri lift, surrounded by wildly muddled rocks; the very sight of this makes climbers' hearts leap. ✿

TOURS

TOUR 1 CINQUE TORRI
Circuit around the Dolomite area of the Cinque Torri, the five towers that are familiar to climbers all over the world. The hike from the parking lot of the chairlift to the bizarre rocks is feasible as a family hike
» 98 ft/760 HM   » 6.2 mi/11 km
» 6 h   » easy

TOUR 2 MONTE PORE
The secluded, pyramid-shaped summit, part of the Averau-Nuvolau group, has no rock faces, but is grassy on all four sides, sometimes also rocky. Monte Pore is easily to reach from the Giaupass road. Also a nice ski tour in winter
» 2,260 ft/210 m EG   » 3.1 mi/5 km
» 2 h   » medium

From the very beginning of mountaineering, the Rifugio Nuvolau has been known for its breathtaking panorama, which extends from its "box seat" on the Nuvolau summit.

299

ITALY | VENETO | RIFUGIO NUVOLAU

"A sea of summits stretches before us; it's impossible to pick one out and describe it separately. Only a camera could capture our impressions."

This quotation was uttered by Paul Grohmann in 1897 for his work "Hiking in the Dolomites."

RIFUGIO NUVOLAU | VENETO | ITALY

ITALY | SOUTH TYROL

50

The Cordial One

BÜLLELEJOCHHÜTTE (RIFUGIO PIAN DI CENGIA) The largest stone sundial in the whole world is in the Dolomites. Mother Nature created it: As the sun wanders along the Dolomite peaks: Neuner, Zehner, Elfer, Zwölfer, and Einser during the course of the day, the time can be determined in relation to the neighboring peaks. But only if you are in the village of Sesto. It takes about four hours to climb from here to the Büllelejochhütte. Its position between the Zwölfer and Einser makes it seem almost closer to the sky than to the earth.

On clear nights, the stars sparkle intoxicatingly beautifully in the sky above the Sesto Dolomites. A peaceful silence settles over the smallest hut in the Drei Zinnen Nature Park, something people do not suspect in the busy hustle and bustle of the day. Spending a night in such an environment feels like taking a trip to another world. It seems that there is actually something about the proximity to the sky here.

The Büllelejochhütte is easy to reach; it's at the foot of the Oberbachernspitze. It is therefore no wonder that the hut's sprawling sun terrace is very busy during the day. Not only does the view of the dreamlike alpine panorama entice people, the hut is the best starting point for numerous tours of varying degrees of difficulty. Whether sporty alpine climbing, spectacular

Nestled in the mountain peaks of the Sesto Dolomites, you feel closer to the sky than to the earth at the little Büllelejochhütte.

ITALY | SOUTH TYROL | BÜLLELEJOCHHÜTTE

via ferrata ascents, or relaxed hikes in front of the unique backdrop of the Großvenediger, Großglockner, and Co.—there's something for every taste.

In the summer months, the host couple Greti and Hubert Rogger manage to balance high-turnover mountain tourism with a slower natural experience. They have filled the cozy Büllelejochhütte with the good feeling that immediately embraces everyone who comes here since 1979. In the meantime, hosting has expanded into a family business; the children and their families also spend the summer months here to help out. Father Hubert remains an unshakable oasis of tranquility. This ski instructor from Sesto came here to stay. In the past, he carried 40 kg backpacks full of food up to the hut on the narrow mountain trail twice a day. Today, he does this with a small tractor, also in order to be able to offer his guests a wider range of food. Cooking is traditional Tyrolean and Italian. In the morning you can tank up for

IN BRIEF

VALLEY TOWNS Moos/Sesto

ALTITUDE 8,294 ft/2,528 m above sea level

OPEN June to October

ACCOMMODATIONS 15-bed dormitory

FOOD Half-board guests can choose from Tyrolean dishes and Italian cuisine, as well as a varied salad bar. Daily menu with hot dishes. Breakfast buffet in the morning

GOOD TO KNOW No cell phone reception, cash only, no shower and generally little available water

BÜLLELEJOCHHÜTTE | SOUTH TYROL | ITALY

In the cloud-covered Drei Zinnen National Park, a sign points in the right direction.

Lightly caramelized, the "sweet omelet," as Kaiserschmarrn is called in Italian, tastes particularly good at the Büllelejochhütte. (top) The trail to the hut takes hikers through a barren rocky landscape. (below)

the day thanks to the breakfast buffet. Special moments await when the day tourists have already gone home and the sun slowly disappears behind the high mountain peaks. Nestled in its small cave, the Büllelejochhütte is waiting for whatever the night will bring. Not infrequently, heavy summer thunderstorms pound this region, accompanied by torrential rains. Anyone who is at home up here will be used to this. Rare native plants such as Dolomites' finger cabbage, yellow yarrow, crocuses, and bellflowers enjoy the moisture. Marmots and deer, black woodpeckers and golden eagles retreat into their shelters and wait until it clears up again and the stars begin to sparkle again. ✺

TOURS

TOUR 1 OBERNACHERNSPITZE
Büllelejochhütte → Mittlerer Oberbachern-spitze on trail 101A; best at sunrise or sunset
» 482 ft/147 m EG » 0.43 mi/700 m
» 0.75 h » easy

TOUR 2 DREI-ZINNEN-HÜTTE
Hike directly to the hut or take the trail via the Paternsattel and Lavaredohütte
» 1,010 ft/308 m EG » 1.9 mi/3.1 km
» 1.5 h » medium

TOUR 3 DREI-ZINNEN CIRCUIT
4-day circuit tour from and to the Fischleinboden parking lot; includes the most famous peak in the Dolomites
» 5,085 ft/1,550 m EG » 16 mi/26 km
» 11 h » medium

■ ITALY | SOUTH TYROL | BÜLLELEJOCHHÜTTE

On the trail of war

To this day, the past lives around the Büllelejochhütte. It's not just shelters, trails and trenches that serve as silent witnesses of the First World War, when the 372-mile front of the mountain war between Austria-Hungary and Italy was waged in the region between Paternkofel and the Drei Zinnen. The so-called Alpini, Italian mountain troops, also left their traces on the terrain when transporting guns and war material with cable cars. Trail 104, which once served as a transport route, is now a hiking trail to a hut.

This black-and-white photograph taken on September 5, 1915 shows an Italian Alpini camp located in the Dolomites at 8,202 feet.

BÜLLELEJOCHHÜTTE | SOUTH TYROL | ITALY

 # SLOVENIA

Slovenia and Liechtenstein have something in common: Both are often forgotten when talking about the Alpine countries. The Triglav region in particular is a paradise for hikers and climbers. Full of lakes and bursting with lush green vegetation, the landscape has a primordial yet gentle side.

Slovenia's hiking trails are usually well-marked, you just have to get used to not always being able to pronounce everything correctly due to the special letters. Hospitality is very important here and hikers' efforts are usually rewarded with hearty traditional dishes. If you want to get to know a new side of the Alps, Slovenia should be the next destination on your bucket list.

Efforts to protect the region around Triglav and Mangart have been underway since the beginning of the 20th century. Today, the Triglav National Park is one of the country's highlights.

51

The Lake Hut

KOČA PRI TRIGLAVSKIH JEZERIH

In the Slovenian Triglav National Park, one of the oldest and most impressive parks in Europe, nature lovers and hiking enthusiasts will find a true paradise. One of the most beautiful hikes does not actually lead to the mighty Trivglav, but into the idyllic valley of the Seven Lakes, where the Koča pri Triglavskih Jetzerih Hut is located.

Although we made it to the summit of Triglav, the highest point in Slovenia at 9,396 feet, we remember everything that came after the ascent better than the ascent itself. This mountain is a kind of sanctuary for the Slovenians. This should become clear at the latest when you look at the crowds of people who are making a pilgrimage to the summit, and so it is not surprising that sometimes there are even traffic jams on the ridge.

However, the picturesque Valley of the Seven Lakes, which is named after the lakes that do not dry out during the summer months, has remained etched in our memory. Because most visitors to the Triglav National Park prefer to follow in the footsteps of its legendary namesake, we have the shadow kingdom in the south of Triglav all to ourselves. The magnificent Seven Lakes Tour, which starts in Stara Fužina on Lake Bohinj and leads across the Voje pastures into a backdrop of mountain pines, boulders, mountain flowers and chamois, takes us to our destination, the Koča pri Triglavskih jezerih Hut. We have already read a lot about this hut, which was built in the

The turquoise lakes that surround this hut invite you to dangle your tired feet in the clear water, especially after a sunny hike.

SLOVENIA | GORENJSKA | KOČA PRI TRIGLAVSKIH JEZERIH HUT

19th century by an Austrian hiking club. The hike is described as particularly worthwhile in many tour books about the Triglav area. And these authors aren't making an empty promise: Slowly the gray rock gives way, and the lush green gets the upper hand. The landscape is a true blessing for the eyes. Located on Double Lake, there is lush flora around the hut, so we admire the Turk's cap lily, yellow gentian, and much more. A special plant here in the National Park is the Dolomites' cinquefoil, also called the Triglav rose, which grows exclusively in the Southern Alps.

The hut itself is a cozy place. You can enjoy the sun here—when it shines. You can't see very far across the landscape since you are not on a summit; the hut is flanked by natural coniferous forests. However, the view of the two lakes between which the hut was built is at least as beautiful as the view from a summit.

IN BRIEF

VALLEY TOWN Ukanc

ALTITUDE 5,528 ft/1,685 m above sea level

OPEN only in the summer from mid-June to the end of September

ACCOMMODATIONS 30 beds in 13 rooms; 170 beds in 13 dormitories; 18 winter beds

FOOD simple dishes: Slovenian specialties

GOOD TO KNOW In case of rain, avoid the direct climb to the hut and instead choose a bypass, which is much longer, but less muddy and slippery.

KOČA PRI TRIGLAVSKIH JEZERIH HUT | GORENJSKA | SLOVENIA

There isn't always bright sunshine in the mountains. You should always keep an eye on the weather; after all, you are not quite as skillful a climber as the chamois.

The hut team's hospitality is refreshing, as is the possibility to fill your water bottle free of charge. This service isn't always offered in other huts. You can recover from the ascent with a cold beer here. However, with around 200 beds, the hut is also comparatively large.

One thing's for certain: We would like to come back and explore the National Park a bit more.

TOURS

TOUR 1 VIA ALPINA
Red Trail: hike to the Štapce saddle across an idyllicplateau dotted with mountain huts to the Pršivec and reach the Koča na Doliču pod Triglavom »2,119 ft/646 m EG »4.7 mi/7.6 km »3 h » medium

TOUR 2 JULIUS-KUGY-DREILÄNDERWEG
Explore Slovenia's mountain landscape. The crossing of the Planina Na polju and the view from the Krn are impressive »4,265 ft/1,300 m EG »12 mi/19.6 km »8 h » medium

When hiking, it's worth looking back at the picturesque hut located between the lakes.

HUT BOOK

Hut host: How do you become one? And if you do, what then?

There are several huts in the Eastern Alps that have been in family hands for decades. For example, the Reinstadler family hosts the Düsseldorfer Hütte; then there's the Siller family in the Nürnberger Hütte and the Fankhausers in the Franz-Senn-Hütte. Most of the time, people work in different huts for a few years until they dare to become hosts. That's how Corina, the host of the Gamshütte, got where she is now. However, there are also exceptions. Sometimes you simply decide to leave everything behind, give up your profession, and become a hut host. For a long time, the Gufferthütte was run by one of these "dropout pairs," with great success. In Switzerland, an official SAC hut maintenance course prepares people for hosting. Then nothing can go wrong.

Preparing food is an important task that requires good planning, because when you run out of something in a hut, the nearest supermarket is not just around the corner.

SLOVENIA | GORENJSKA

52

The Original One

It's not only the two-legged guests who feel comfortable on the grounds of Češka Koča; sheep also enjoy the lush green surrounding the hut.

ČEŠKA KOČA For more than 120 years, the Češka Koča has perched below the Grintovec, the highest peak in the Steiner Alps. Although it has been renovated several times since its opening, it has never lost its original charm.

Dedicated on June 26, 1900, the Češka Koča—or Czech hut—is the oldest hut in Slovenia. It was built by the Czech branch of the Slovenian Alpine Association, to which it owes its name.

From the campsite near Jezersko, we hike on the road through the Ravenska Valley to the hut's material cableway. From here, a hiking trail takes us up to the Češka Koča, which has stood in its magnificent location on the oval cirque of the Spodnja Raven for over 120 years. We decided to try the hiking trail, but a very difficult via ferrata offers an alternative if you're a climber.

In contrast to the time when it was built, this small hut now has an electrical connection. In addition, there are modern washrooms and even a shower on the hut's lower level. However, the outside of the hut has hardly changed. It is still a cute, cozy, and very original hut that resembles a Bohemian farmhouse. Its location on the slope means that you have a wonderful view of the Kočna Valley. But the panoramic view of Baba and Rinka is also impressive.

The Steiner Alps are a small mountain range in northern Slovenia near the Austrian border. This area is extremely varied and offers exciting via ferrata routes. So our task the next day will be to cross the Grintovec, the highest summit in the range. From the hut we head south into a cirque, which soon leads to a steep

317

SLOVENIA | GORENJSKA | ČEŠKA KŎCA

rock slope. Quite exposed, we crawl up the shady north flank, where the most difficult passages feature steel ropes and pegs. A path takes us up to the ridge between Kočna and Grintovec and after the Dolskra skrbina ridge, there's the ascent to Grintovec. Here, too, the steepest points are secured. We climb these without any problems thanks to our mountaineering experience, and we soon reach the highest point of the Steiner Alps and enjoy the panoramic view from this magnificent summit.

And because we haven't had enough yet, we decide to climb the Skuta summit, which is only 85 feet lower than the Grintovec. Once we reach the top, we bask in the sun again before proceeding on to the shady north side.

In the evening, as soon as the sun sets, the landscape feels a bit inhospitable, so we are happy to reach the hut. We have set aside three days for our trip to the Steiner Alps, so we will spend a relaxed night in the hut.

IN BRIEF

VALLEY TOWN Jezersko

ALTITUDE 5,059 ft/1,542 m above sea level

OPEN May to mid-June on weekends and mid-June to end of September

ACCOMMODATIONS 33 beds in multi-bed rooms, 20-bed dormitory, 6-bed winter room

FOOD Delicious, traditional food, the breakfast is especially good

GOOD TO KNOW It's also possible to reach the hut via a difficult via ferrata.

ČEŠKA KOČA | GORENJSKA | SLOVENIA

The paths are well-marked, so knowing where you are when you're hiking is not difficult.

In the evening, the hut's host pampers us with delicious Slovenian cuisine. Goulash soup and the like quickly ensure that the day's tribulations are forgotten. And the team will also do their best to make your stay as pleasant as possible, not least because of their friendly manner and organizational talent. So, well-fed and in a good mood, we can look back on our great crossing once again and anticipate the comfortable beds.

TOURS

TOUR 1 JULIUS-KUGY-DREILÄNDERWEG
6th stage goes past the hut. Kamniška koča → Zgornje Jezersko. Old road replaced by the "Slovenska Pot"
» 2,658 ft/810 m EG » 7.6 mi/12.3 km
» 7.5 h » difficult

TOUR 2 VIA FERRATA ČESCKA KOČA
New via ferrata is difficult! Just 2 minutes from the path to the hut
» 1,050 ft/320 m EG » 8.08 mi/980 m
» 1 h » difficult

TOUR 3 GRINTOVEC
Hut is ideal start for the tour of the Grintovec through the Ravni Kar mountain basin and the Mlinarsko sedlo
» 3,051 ft/930 m EG » 1.9 mi/3 km
» 3 h » difficult

Chamois, edelweiss, and alpine buttercup may draw your attention at the trail's edge.

SLOVENIA | GORENJSKA | ČEŠKA KOČA

Mountaineering villages

The Alpine Associations' Mountaineering Villages initiative honors original mountain villages, where mountains and mountaineering are part of the cultural self-image. These are places that invite you to enjoy and linger, and they represent sustainable development in the Alpine region. Jezersko, the starting point for Česka Koča, was the first mountaineering village in Slovenia. A cultural highlight are the many 16th-century farmsteads that are still preserved in the village.

From Mount Krn you can see a lush green landscape of meadows and forests and the individual houses of a small village in the Triglav National Park.

ČEŠKA KŎCA | GORENJSKA | SLOVENIA

Large herds of impressive animals are living in the Alps once again. Ibex had disappeared completely in Bavaria by the middle of the 19th century, but they have been brought back from the edge of extinction.

HUTS WITH CHARACTER

INDEX

A
Adlerweg 121
Aiguille de Bionnassay 31
Aiguille du Goûter 31
Aiguille du Moine 39
Aiguille du Plan 35
Ailefroide 18
All'Acqua 76
Alpine marmots 212
Alta Badia 290
Anton-Karg-Haus 215
Aperer Turm 187
Appenzell 92ff.
Auberge du Truc 23
Austria 140ff.
Auvergne-Rhône-Alpes 22ff.

B
Bad Reichenhall 136
Bärentrek 59
Bavaria 108ff.
Bayerwald bei Kreuth 130
Becherhaus 255
Bedretto 76
Berggasthaus Schäfler 93
Bergsteigerdörfer 320
Berliner Hütte
Bern 46ff., 68ff.
Birgsau 108
Biwak 265
Blinnenhorn 77
Blüemlisalphütte 57
Bordierhütte 65
Botzer 255
Brandenburger Haus 155
Bremer Hütte 191
Brixner Hütte 283
Buchstein 131
Büllelejochhütte 303

C
Česka koča 317
Cancellation 11
Capanna Corno Gries 75
Capanna Regina
Margherita 244

Carinthia 224ff.
Chamonix 34
Chamonix-Mont-Blanc 38
Cinque Torri 299
Coburger Hütte 171
Cortina d'Ampezzo 298
Cresta della Croce 235

D
Dakota C-53 72
Dauphiné Alps 17ff.
Delicacies 165
Doldenhorn 49, 53
Doldenhornhütte 47
Drei-Zinnen-Hütte 305
Drei-Zinnen Circuit 305
Durnholz 260
Durnholzer See 260
Düsseldorfer Hütte 239

E
Ehrwald 172
Ernst-Riml-Spitze 177
Erzherzog-Johann-Hütte 227
Eschenlohe 118
Ewigschneehorn 71

F
Falkenhütte 193
Fanatkogel 221
Fane 266
Farchant 118
Fauna 295
Feichten im Kaunertal 156
Finkenberg 200
Firmisanschneide 169
Flaggerschartenhütte 259
France 14ff.
Franz-Senn-Hütte 185
Friesenberghaus 201
Fründenhorn 53
Fründenhütte 51, 59
Fürstin-Gina-Weg 103

G
Gamshütte 199
Gamsjoch 195
Gardeccia (Trento) 274

Garmisch-Partenkirchen 112, 118
Gartlhütte 273
Gaulihütte 69
Germany 104ff.
Ginzling 206, 210
Glocknerrunde 227
Gorenjska 310ff.
Gorezmettlenbach 82
Grasleiten Circuit 281
Graubünden 86ff.
Greizer Hütte 209
Gries im Sulztal 176
Grieshorn 77
Grinbergspitzen 201
Grintovec 319
Großer Löffler 211
Großer Mörchner 207
Großglockner 221, 228
Gufferthütte 131
Gumpenkar 125
Gurtnellen Village 83

H
Hangendgletscherhorn 71
Heiligenblut 226
Heuberg Panorama Trail 53
Hintereisspitzen 157
Hinterer Spiegelkogel 169
Hinterer Tajakopf 173
Hinteres Schöneck 241
Hinterriß 194
Hochlandhütte 125
Hochwanner 113
Hohe Geige 163
Hoher Angelus 241
Horseshoe Tour 261
Hospitality 12
Hütten-Knigge 203
Hut guestbook 12
Hut host 315

I
Ice parade 256
Innere Sommerwand 187
Innertkirchen 70
Italy 230ff.

J
Jakobsspitze 261
Jegertosse 49
Jezersko 318
Julius-Kugy-Dreiländerweg 313, 319

K
Kaiser-Franz-Josefs-Höhe 226
Kaiserschützensteig 217
Kals am Großglockner 220, 226
Kaltenberghütte 149
Kandersteg 48, 52, 58
Karwendel Tour 195
Kasseler Hütte 211
Kesselkogel 275
Kesselwandspitze 157
Klais 118
Kleinbärenzinne 163
Kleines Seehorn 145
Kleinlitzner 145
Koča pri Triglavskih Jezerih 311
Kolfuschg 290
Konstanzer Hütte 151
Krachelspitze 151
Krapfenkar 125
Kreuzeckhaus 113
Kronenwanderung 89
Krottenkopf 119
Krün 118, 124
Kufstein 216
Kuhflucht Waterfalls 119

L
La Nonne 39
Ladin 292
Lago di Luzzone 89
Langen 150
Langtalereckhütte 169
Lenggrieser Hütte 131
Lenzspitze 65
Liechtenstein 98
Lobbia Alta 235
Losenheim 260

M
Mädelegabel 109
Mahnkopf 195
Mairspitze 191
Malbun 102
Mankei 212
Martell 248
Maximilian via ferrata 281
Mer de Glace 39
Mischabelhütte 63, 65
Mittelstaufen 137
Mittewald 260
Mont Blanc 25, 31, 35
Mont Pelvoux 19
Monte Cevedale 249
Monte Pore 299
Monte-Rosa-Hütte 43
Moos 304
Müllerhütte 253
Murmele via ferrata 249

N
Nadelhorn 65
Neustift im Stubaital 186
Nürnberger Hütte 189

O
Oberau 118
Oberbärgli 49
Obergurgl im Ötztal 168
Obernachernspitze 305
Öhrlikopf 95
Ötzi 178

P
Packing list 13
Partenen 144
Payer, Julius 242
Payment 11
Pfälzerhütte 101
Pfunderer Höhenweg 285
Piding 136
Pisciadù Hütte 289
Piz Boè 291
Piz Vial 89
Plangeross 162
Plattkofelhütte 281
Plima Schluchtenweg 249

INDEX

The Alpine edelweiss is not only famous, it embodies the Alpine regions and serves as an important symbol there.

Provence-Alpes-Côte d'Azur 16ff.
Puchberg 260

R
Ramolhaus 167
Ranalt 190
Rappenseehütte 109
Rauhekopfhütte 157
Refuge de la Balme 25
Refuge de Tête Rousse 29
Refuge des Cosmiques 33
Refuge du Couvercle 37
Refuge du Pelvoux 17
Reichenhaller Haus 135
Reintalangerhütte 111
Reservations 11
Ridnaun-Maiern 254
Rifugio Alpe di Tires 278
Rifugio Bolzano 266
Rifugio Bressanone 282
Rifugio Cima Libera 252
Rifugio Forcella Vallaga 258
Rifugio Franco Cavazza al Pisciadù 288
Rifugio Lobbia Alta 233
Rifugio Mandrone 235

Rifugio Nino Corsi 247
Rifugio Nuvolau 297
Rifugio Pian di Cengia 302
Rifugio Re Alberto I 272
Rifugio Serristori 238
Rüsselsheimer Hütte 161

S
Saarbrücker Hütte 143
Saas Fee 64
Saint-Gervais-les-Bains 24, 30
Salmhütte 225
Santnerpasssteig 275
Schachtkopf 173
Schalfkogel 169
Scheiblehnkogel 183
Schere 221
Schlernhaus 267
Schönau Passeier 254
Schönbichler Horn 207
Schöttelkarspitze 125
Seealpsee 95
Seis am Schlern 280
Seiser Alm 269
Sellrainer Hüttenrunde 177
Sewenhütte 81
Sexten 304

Siegerlandhütte 181
Slovenia 308ff.
Soiernhaus 123
Sölden im Ötztal 182
Sonklarspitze 183
Sonneck 217
Sonnenspitzrunde 173
South Tyrol 238, 302ff.
St. Christoph 150
Stabelerturm 275
Stripsenjochhaus 217
Stubaier Höhenweg 191
Stuben am Arlberg 150
Stüdlhütte 219
Sulden 240
Sulzenau Hütte 191
Sumvitg 88
Sustlihütte 83
Switzerland 44ff.

T
Tagewaldhorn 261
Tegernseer Hütte 129
Terrihütte 87
Tessin 74ff.
Tierser Alplhütte 279
Tiroler Höhenweg 121
Tour du Mont Blanc 25

Transalp 121
Trettachspitze 109
Trento 232ff.
Triesenberg 100ff.
Tschafonhütte 269
Tschenglser Hochwand 241
Tübinger Hütte 145
Tyrol 154ff.

U
Ukanc 312
Uri 80ff.

V
Val di Genova 234
Val Gardena Circuit 291
Vals 284
Veneto 296ff.
Vent im Ötztal 156
Verwall Round 151
Via Alpina 103, 121, 313
Via ferrata Česka koča 319
Via Weißbier 132
Vier-Quellen-Weg 77
Völs am Schlern 268
Vorarlberg 142ff.
Vordere Sommerwand 187

W
Walgau 118
Wallis 64ff.
Waltenbergerhaus 107
Wankhaus 119
Wasserauen 94
Wasserfallweg 71
Weilheimer Hütte 117
Weißmurachsee 163
Welschnofen (South Tyrol) 274
Wiener Höhenweg 227
Wilde Kreuzspitze 285
Wilder See 285
Wildi Frau 59
Windachtal Hut Tour 183
Winnebachseehütte 175

Z
Zsigmondyspitze 207
Zuckerhütl 255
Zufallhütte 247
Zugspitze 113
Zwergenweg 83
Zwieselalm 137

325

The view from the mountaintop—here from the autumnal Bischofsmütze—is worth the strenuous ascent.

PHOTO CREDITS/IMPRINT

A = Alamy; C = Corbis; G = Getty; M = Mauritius Images

Cover: Front: Look/Bernard van Dierendonck; back: Getty/Westend61
p. 2 Diego Gaspari Bandion; p. 4 G/Glenn Pettersen; p. 9 G/Uwe Umstätter; p. 10 Look/Christoph Jorda; p. 13 Look/Bernard van Dierendonck; p. 13 Look/Andreas Strau; p. 14-15 G/Mario Colonel; p. 16-17 Mathieu Jaudon; p. 18-19 Look/Andreas Strau; p. 19 G/Alun Richardson; p. 20-21 M/David Pickford; p. 22-23 M/Alamy; p. 24-25 Look/Tobias Richter; p. 26-27 G/Buena Vista Images; p. 28-29 M/Stefan Auth; p. 30 M/Alamy; p. 31 M/Alamy; p. 32-33 M/Alamy; p. 34 M/Alamy; p. 35 M/Bernd Ritschel; p. 36-37 M/Jean-François Hagenmuller; p. 38 M/Moritz Wolf; p. 038-039 Look/ClickAlps; p. 40-41 Renata Sedmakova/Shutterstock.com; p. 42-43 Look/Bernard van Dierendonck; p. 44-45 C/Michele Falzone; p. 46-47 A/GFC Collection; p. 48 M/AIC; p. 48 G/Fredy Jeanrenaud; p. 49 G/Cdbr Photography; p. 50-51 A/GFC Collection; p. 52 Look/Daniel Schoenen; p. 52 Look/Iris Ker; p. 53 Look/Daniel Schoenen; p. 54-55 Look/Christoph Jorda; p. 56-57 M/Marcel Gross; p. 58 M/ImageBroker; p. 58-59 Look/Iris Ker; p. 59 Look/Iris Ker; p. 60-61 G/Stockbyte; p. 62-63 M/Alamy; p. 64 Look/Caroline Fink; p. 64-65 Look/Ralf Gantzhorn; p. 66-67 M/Alamy; p. 68-69 Look/Caroline Fink; p. 70 G/Mercedes Catalan; p. 71 A/Dukas Presseagentur; p. 72-73 A/Dukas Presseagentur; p. 74-75 Look/Andreas Strauß; p. 76 Look/Andreas Strauß; p. 77 M/Alamy; p. 78-79 Minbarian/Shutterstock.com; p. 80-81 Look/Bernard van Dierendonck; p. 82 Look/Bernard van Dierendonck; p. 83 Look/Bernard van Dierendonck; p. 84-85 Sheryl Watson/Shutterstock.com; p. 86-87 M/Armin Mathis; p. 88 M/Roland Schmid; p. 89 M/Raphael Weber; p. 90-91 M/Armin Mathis; p. 92-93 Look/ClickAlps; p. 94 Look/Daniel Schoenen; p. 95 G/Increativemedia; p. 96-97 M/Nicolas Alexander Otto; p. 98-99 G/Alexander J.E. Bradley; p. 100-101 M/Wolfgang Berroth; p. 102 M/BY; p. 102-103 M/Busse & Yankushev; p. 104-105 M/Stefan Hefele; p. 106-107 DAV Sektion Allgäu-Immenstadt; p. 108 Look/Andreas Strauß; p. 109 Look/Andreas Strauß; p. 110-111 Look/Andreas Strauß; p. 112 Look/Jan Greune; p. 112-113 G/Seen by hotshot; p. 114-115 Look/Ludwig Mallaun; p. 116-117 M/Christa Eder; p. 118 M/Klaus Neuner; p. 118-119 M/Christa Eder; p. 120-121 G/Uwe Umstätter; p. 122-123 M/Volker Dautzenberg; p. 124 Look/Andreas Strauß; p. 125 M/Christine Braun; p. 126-127 G/Heritage Images; p. 128-129 Look/Andreas Strauß; p. 130 Look/Andreas Strauß; p. 131 M/Alamy; p. 132-133 M/ImageBroker; p. 134-135 Look/Andreas Strauß; p. 136 M/Christian Back; p. 136 M/Josef Kuchlbauer; p. 137 M/Hans Fürmann; p. 138-139 M/Bernd Ritschel; p. 140-141 G/Alfons Hauke; p. 142-143 M/Roland T. Frank; p. 144 G/Arto Hakola; p. 145 M/Martin Siepmann; p. 145 M/Matthias Pinn; p. 146-147 G/University of Southern California; p. 148-149 M/Busse & Yankushev; p. 150 M/Bruno Kickner; p. 150 M/Reinhard Hölzl; p. 151 M/Ludwig Mallaun; p. 152-153 M/Ludwig Mallaun; p. 154-155 A/Allan Hartley; p. 156-157 Look/Andreas Strauß; p. 158-159 G/Dino židov; p. 160-161 M/Timm Humpfer; p. 162 M/Bernd Ritschel; p. 162 G/Gerhard Kraus; p. 163 M/Bernd Ritschel; p. 164-165 M/Alamy; p. 166-167 M/Timm Humpfer; p. 168 M/Timm Humpfer; p. 168 M/Timm Humpfer; p. 169 M/Timm Humpfer; p. 170-171 Jürgen Schranz; p. 172 Look/Andreas Strauß; p. 173 M/Alamy; p. 174-175 M/Timm Humpfer; p. 176 M/Timm Humpfer; p. 177 M/Timm Humpfer; p. 178-179 G/Kean Collection; p. 180-181 M/Bernd Ritschel; p. 182 M/Timm Humpfer; p. 183 M/Bernd Ritschel; p. 184-185 Look/Andreas Strauß; p. 186 M/Alamy; p. 186 M/Alamy; p. 187 Look/Andreas Strauß; p. 188-189 M/Bernd Ritschel; p. 190 M/Timm Humpfer; p. 191 Look/Andreas Strauß; p. 192-193 Look/Andreas Strauß; p. 194 M/Nico Hermann; p. 194-195 M/Thomas Schöpf; p. 196 Sektion Oberland des DAV e.V.; p. 196 Sektion Oberland des DAV e.V.; p. 197 Sektion Oberland des DAV e.V.; p. 197 Sektion Oberland des DAV e.V.; p. 198-199 Thomas Rychly; p. 200 Look/Robertharding; p. 201 M/Dan Kollmann; p. 202-203 G/Imagno; p. 204-205 A/Allan Hartley; p. 206 A/Matthias Riedinger; p. 206 Look/Andreas Strau; p. 207 M/Moritz Wolf; p. 208-209 M/Moritz Wolf; p. 210 M/Alamy; p. 210 G/ImageBroker; p. 211 M/Alamy; p. 212-213 Look/age; p. 214-215 Look/Lukas Larsson; p. 216 Look/Lukas Larsson; p. 217 Look/Lukas Larsson; p. 218-219 M/Gerhard Wild; p. 220 Look/Hermann; p. 221 Look/Andreas Strauß; p. 222-223 G/Imagno; p. 223 Look/Andreas Strauß; p. 224-225 A/Christian Peters; p. 226 M/Volker Preusser; p. 227 G/Dieter Meyrl; p. 228 M/Alamy; p. 229 G/Imagno; p. 230-231 G/Anita Stizzoli; p. 232-233 Look/Reinhard Dirscherl; p. 234 Look/Andreas Strauß; p. 234 Look/Andreas Strauß; p. 235 Look/Andreas Strauß; p. 236-237 M/Memento; p. 238-239 Düsseldorfer Hütte; p. 240 G/Martin Braito; p. 240 M/Guenter Fischer; p. 241 Düsseldorfer Hütte; p. 242-243 M/Alamy; p. 244-245 A/Roberto Spampinato; p. 246-247 Picasa; p. 248 Picasa; p. 248 Picasa; p. 249 Helmuth Rier; p. 250-251 M/Robert Jank; p. 252-253 M/Martin Braito; p. 254 M/Martin Braito; p. 255 M/Martin Braito; p. 256-257 Look/Jan Greune; p. 258-259 M/Alamy; p. 260-261 Look/Andreas Strauß; p. 262-263 G/Hwo; p. 264-265 Look/Andreas Strauß; p. 266-267 Look/ClickAlps; p. 268 G/Westend61; p. 269 M/Gerhard Nixdorf; p. 270-271 Look/Lukas Larsson; p. 272-273 G/Paolo Bis; p. 274 G/Mara Brandl; p. 275 M/Massimiliano Broggi; p. 276-277 M/ClickAlps; p. 278-279 Look/ClickAlps; p. 280 M/Reinhard Hölzl; p. 280 M/Reinhard Hölzl; p. 280-281 M/Roberto Moiola; p. 282-283 Wolfgang Oberhofer; p. 284 G/Sandra Schmid; p. 285 M/ImageBroker; p. 286-287 M/Wolfgang Weinhäupl; p. 288-289 M/ClickAlps; p. 290 M/Alamy; p. 291 M/Alamy; p. 292-293 M/Pitopia; p. 294-295 Sheryl Watson/Shutterstock.com; p. 296-297 M/Mikolaj Gospodarek; p. 298-299 Giacomo Pompanin; p. 300-301 M/Annett Schmitz; p. 302-303 M/Alamy; p. 304 A/age; p. 304 A/ago; p. 305 A/ago; p. 306 307 G/De Agostini Picture Library; p. 308-309 M/Stefan Hefele; p. 310-311 A/ImageBroker; p. 312 A/ImageBroker; p. 313 G/Bosca78; p. 314-315 Look/Bernard van Dierendonck; p. 316-317 Primož Šenk; p. 318 M/Roland T. Frank; p. 318 M/Alamy; p. 318 M/Martin Siepmann; p. 319 Drejc Karniar; p. 320-321 Look/Cavan Images; p. 322 Look/Reinhard Hölzl; p. 325 G/Frans Schalekamp; p. 326 G/Christoph Oberschneider / EyeEm

Text: Katinka Holupirek, Janina Meier, Markus Meier, Annika Voigt
Translation: Dr. Linda Gaus
Type set in: Frutiger, Kepler, Olicana, URW DIN

© 2024 Kunth Verlag – MAIRDUMONT GmbH & Co. KG, Ostfildern, Germany
Library of Congress Control Number: 2024930416

All rights reserved. No part of this work may be reproduced or used in any form or by any means—graphic, electronic, or mechanical, including photocopying or information storage and retrieval systems—without written permission from the publisher. The scanning, uploading, and distribution of this book or any part thereof via the Internet or any other means without the permission of the publisher is illegal and punishable by law. Please purchase only authorized editions and do not participate in or encourage the electronic piracy of copyrighted materials.

"Schiffer," "Schiffer Publishing, Ltd.," and the pen and inkwell logo are registered trademarks of Schiffer Publishing, Ltd.

ISBN: 978-0-7643-6805-9
Printed in China

Published by Schiffer Publishing, Ltd.
4880 Lower Valley Road
Atglen, PA 19310
Phone: (610) 593-1777; Fax: (610) 593-2002
info@schifferbooks.com
www.schifferbooks.com

For our complete selection of fine books on this and related subjects, please visit our website at www.schifferbooks.com. You may also write for a free catalog.
Schiffer Publishing's titles are available at special discounts for bulk purchases for sales promotions or premiums. Special editions, including personalized covers, corporate imprints, and excerpts, can be created in large quantities for special needs. For more information, contact the publisher.